RUST BELT BOY

RUST BELT BOY

Stories of an American Childhood

Paul Hertneky

BAUHAN PUBLISHING

PETERBOROUGH NEW HAMPSHIRE

2016

ISBN 978-087233-222-5

Library of Congress Cataloging-in-Publication Data
Names: Hertneky, Paul, author.
Title: Rust Belt boy : stories of an American childhood / Paul Hertneky.
Description: Peterborough, New Hampshire : Bauhan Publishing, [2016]
Identifiers: LCCN 2015049926 | ISBN 9780872332225 (pbk. : alk. paper)
Subjects: LCSH: Hertneky, Paul. | Ambridge (Pa.)--Biography. | Iron and steel
workers--Pennsylvania--Pittsburgh--Biography. | Pittsburgh (Pa.)--Social
life and customs--20th century. |
Students--Pennsylvania--Pittsburgh--Biography. | Baby boom
generation--Pennsylvania--Pittsburgh--Biography. | Working
class--Pennsylvania--Pittsburgh--Social life and customs--20th century.
Classification: LCC F159.A55 H47 2016 | DDC 974.8/86043092--dc23
LC record available at http://lccn.loc.gov/2015049926

Book design by Kirsty Anderson.
Typeset in Minion Pro.
Cover design by Eugenia Kim and Henry James.
Author photo by Joanna Eldredge Morrissey; used with permission.

Manufactured by Versa Press.

BAUHAN
PUBLISHING LLC
PO BOX 117 PETERBOROUGH NEW HAMPSHIRE 03458
603-567-4430
WWW.BAUHANPUBLISHING.COM

MANUFACTURED IN THE UNITED STATES

For Robbie

In Memory
Elizabeth Hertneky
Milton Hertneky
and
Denise Antkiewicz Hertneky

CONTENTS

We were vaguely proud of living in a city so full of distinct immigrant groups, among which we never thought to number ourselves. We had no occasion to visit the steep hillside neighborhoods—Polish, Hungarian, Rumanian, Italian, Slav—of the turn-of-the-century immigrants who poured the steel, and stirred the glass and shoveled the coal.

ANNIE DILLARD
on Pittsburgh, in *An American Childhood*

1

A Turning Tide

Most of the essays and stories I've written about growing up in Ambridge, Pennsylvania, the details of life in a steel town, with its ethnic enclaves and round-the-clock factories, I relegated to a file while the surrounding industrial heartland crumbled. Returning to this once-illustrious plateau and its steep hillside neighborhoods, fifteen miles upriver from Pittsburgh, broke my heart as the nation averted its eyes from the economic disaster sweeping across the Great Lakes in the 1980s and 90s, taking Ambridge with it. Unemployed workers poured into Sun Belt cities, and the places they abandoned were so widespread their stories became a sad cliché. I kept my drafts in a drawer. If I were going to look at them again, the tide would have to turn.

One day in 2005, my father pointed out an item in *The Beaver County Times* about an Australian developer and his interests in the town's brownfields—polluted post-industrial tracts the Environmental Protection Agency (EPA) identified as available for sale and federal matching funds for the cost of cleaning them up. But who was the Aussie? I had to meet him. I had an intense interest in anyone who had a vision for my decrepit hometown, some of which was fueled by the natural skepticism natives had already voiced about his grand plan. I worked a few contacts and set up lunch with

Robert Moltoni and his local man on the scene, Mike Bort.

During our meal in a converted silk-making operation from the 1830s in the historic district, Moltoni, a trim, brawny, former brick-peeler from Perth with a nose that travels east to west, ordered a steamed milk, with honey. The young *barista* blanched upon hearing the order, but figured it out quickly enough. I, on the other hand, was speechless.

Metaphors seldom hurl themselves at me like that. Here was a man looking to cash in on 425 acres right in the middle of town that had been built by thousands of immigrants who had been seeking a land of milk and honey. As I set foot outside afterwards, I looked left and thought about the wave of eventual steelworkers who came in 1904, I looked right, straight into a German enclave, built in 1824, and I looked around at this plateau along the Ohio River that George Washington had surveyed for speculation in 1753, noting the excellence of the land and negotiating with the chief of seven Indian tribes who built a commercial center here—right over there—at the end of the 1600s and prospered for more than fifty years.

For three centuries, at least, humans had been coming to this place to make their lives, and in each century, they were led there by a single man, visionaries all. Might Robert Moltoni be the fourth?

"A land flowing with milk and honey" is how it goes in Exodus. In my reading, God had promised the Israelites he would send them to "this most glorious of all lands." (And, they'd better get to it and stay in line or he'd kill them all—but never mind about that.)

As children, we heard very little about the events that had taken place in Ambridge. Our teachers ignored the stories. Our immigrant parents and grandparents showed little interest in local history. It was not *their* history. We were taught to look ahead, not back. Conquer nature, explore the frontier, exploit the resources, manifest destiny; if anything truly important had happened here it would have been included in the textbooks that came from Boston.

In many ways, Ambridge served as a border town between the Northeast and Midwest and always displayed a wild frontier attitude. Men gambled away wives. Children operated bars. Fortune seekers stopped for the night before heading into the vast midlands. Sewickley, its affluent neighbor to the east, turns up its tweedy collars against the winds off the plains, and reverently faces New England. Just to the west, beyond Ambridge, life flattens and spreads out.

Prosperity allowed my grandparents and parents to remain in town with every expectation that succeeding generations would do the same. But my generation's economic prospects fell away at the same time all Americans became more mobile, and ours was a restless generation to begin with. Between 1975 and 1995, half of the baby boomers left hometowns in a swath of geography that runs roughly from Troy, New York, south to Baltimore, west to St. Louis and north to Duluth. When heavy industry began to collapse in the late 1970s, boomers were between fifteen and thirty-five years old—either in the workforce, or about to be. The steel industry alone lost nearly 300,000 jobs in the blink of an eye, setting off a widespread exodus, one that equaled the largest internal migration in US history. Ironically, roughly six million African Americans fled into the north when the industrial revolution began, and the same number of industrial workers moved out when the era ended a hundred years later. But the Great Migration north took fifty years to unfold, whereas the emptying of the Rust Belt took place in only twenty years.

Crash and all, most of my family still lives around Pittsburgh and has watched it rise from the ashes. One upside of relying on a single industry meant that the speed with which it fell affected the speed of its recovery. Pittsburgh hit bottom hard, and has bounced back more quickly than similar cities. In the 1990s, the county surrounding Pittsburgh had the second oldest population in the United States—just behind Palm Beach—and its schools, social welfare, and health systems were forced to innovate. They have, breaking new ground in urban education and devising community medical systems that keep elders near home. Like tempered steel, the locals have been made sharper and stronger through extreme stress.

Those who have moved away often describe feeling a push-and-pull with their hometowns, acknowledging a gravity that keeps them in orbit around their roots. The relationship thrives at a distance, explaining why there are Pittsburgh Steeler bars from Vancouver to Miami and Belfast to Shanghai. They serve as embassies and surrogates for members of what demographer James Russell calls "the Burgh Diaspora," and are the natural result of mass emigration as well as a reminder of how the globalization of an industry can lead to the global pollination of a culture.

Sons and daughters lucky enough to feel attached to a distinct hometown know it works its way under our skin and into our being. Pluck a hair out of my corpse a hundred years from now and DNA evidence will show that I grew up in Ambridge, one place on Earth, starting in 1955. Biologically, I am tied to it, but that's just the beginning.

Nearly all of the following essays and stories are set in Ambridge and Pittsburgh, but every American settlement has seen waves of immigrants. Those waves often come and go without us recognizing their singularity, their influence, and the pattern they follow. I have written these essays to acknowledge the six million boomers who moved away—from Milwaukee and Youngstown and Scranton and all the places in between—and in appreciation for the six million who stayed home and supplied the gravity, took care of the parents, the towns, and each other.

2

Horns in the Hollows

Maybe it's just the wind whistling through my woodshed, but some mornings I swear I hear the air horns from the trains and factories in the Ohio Valley, echoing through the hollows and the decades that have passed. They greet me at the gates of Armco Steel, running full tilt when I turned twenty-one and joined thousands of men and women who filed in and out of the mill three times a day, seven days a week. Throughout the valley, all the mills' horns had a way of keeping time in close measure for those of us working sixty-hour weeks. Like the rivers and rails that hemmed us in, we had no room for deviation and rolled along, punching in and punching out.

Outside the mill, our elbows resting on the edge of a bar, the old guys winked at an inside joke and smokers rocked back and closed their eyes at the end of a long drag on a Marlboro. In the quiet moments, I noticed how the family men sank into a hunch while picking at a longneck label, transfixed by a wooden chit that magically turns into another beer. They looked like they were taking cover, the way a boxer does against the ropes.

This would be the final round for the steel industry in America. We all saw it coming—written in yellow crayon, usually in Asian characters—on the imported billets stacked in the shipping department.

As always, bars and churches held us together, and the streets of Ambridge were thick with both. Every ethnic group had at least one church: Russians, Greeks, Italians, Croatians, Poles, Serbs, Ukrainians, Scots, Czechs and Slovaks, Germans—Catholic and Orthodox mostly, but Baptists, Lutherans, Episcopalians, and Presbyterians too. A bigger, modern synagogue replaced the old one in the 1960s. Belief in God and country, family and football, preserved the hopes of sixteen thousand souls who were welded together by the business of steel and crammed into Ambridge.

When faith faltered, we had bars—hundreds of them in every neighborhood and lining Merchant Street. Even legendary boozehounds who began a pub-crawl anywhere on Merchant, drinking a beer in every joint, would cover no more than three blocks before collapsing on the sidewalk. In those days, Ambridge had more bars and clubs per capita than most anywhere in the nation: Manhattan had one for every six hundred residents, Philadelphia had one for every five hundred, Pittsburgh had one for every four hundred, and Ambridge had twice as many: one for every two hundred.

Taverns, like Maxim's directly across the street from the mill gates, stayed open all day and night. They served workers who were mostly tired and harmless but were not always friends. Some brought axes to grind, bones to pick, and hairs to split, simmering beneath the surface or looking for a fight, if only to feel more alive.

Toby Schmidt had that hateful look on his face, sitting across the horseshoe-shaped bar one morning, boring a hole straight through me. I hadn't noticed him sitting there until I dropped onto a stool, beat after an eleven-to-seven shift. Sunlight knifed through the tiny windows and bounced off the pool table, adding a green cast to Toby's wavy black hair, still slick from his shower. The wiry Carl DeLessio sat next to him, puzzling over dollar bills, steadily losing at liar's poker to the smooth coot at the end of the bar. I looked around for my pals—guys I grew up with—through the dust of the sunbeam in front, down the hall toward the cigarette and pinball machines. I expected them any minute, so I dug into my jeans for money and caught Toby still staring me down.

The bartender, wearing a peasant blouse that set off the freckly tan on her shoulders, stepped between us and smiled. She placed a shot glass in front of me and filled it to the very top with Imperial, cheap whiskey I found too penetrating for a summer morning. "It's from Toby," she said. I could hardly hear her; my ears still ringing from working a jackhammer. I read her lips and followed the jerk of her head to the jerk across the bar.

"A bottle of Iron, please," I probably shouted, sliding a few bills toward her. "And return the favor, okay?" She swung around the island and the cash register and filled his glass. He lifted the shot toward me and stretched a rotten grin across his face. I acknowledged the gesture, threw back the whiskey and chased it with cold beer.

Where were Jack and Lenny? They should have showered and been here by now. Toby hadn't bought me a whiskey to be friendly. He was pissed off, or so I heard in the locker room, and Imperial was his way of settling the score. I felt a pang of wishing I were back in a Pitt college bar, where nobody threw gauntlets all too common in bars like this one. The goal was to force me to drink or refuse his generosity, which he would take as an insult. He was older, about thirty, heavier, a big drinker with high tolerance. I was a stringbean kid. Going shot-for-shot, I'd fall off my stool before his cheeks turned rosy.

It had started seven hours earlier, as Emil Sammartino

and I stood before a mound of curly steel shavings that were congealed in oil, waste created by cutting threads in the ends of pipe. We were shoveling it into a crane bucket, a steel box half the size of a dumpster. Each shovelful weighed about fifty pounds. Emil and I held the lowest status of the roughly twenty-five hundred workers at Armco and we often laughed out of disbelief at the tasks we faced. We paced ourselves, knowing we'd be at it all night.

Toby, whose job elsewhere in the mill had been canceled, appeared in the shadow of a foreman who didn't like him. He had a reputation for sucking up and slacking off. Until he could be reassigned, Toby was told to help Emil and me.

Fuck this, he spat, after lifting two shovelfuls. And he headed off to take a leak. We figured we'd seen the last of him for a while, and we were right. Before lunchtime, the foreman came by looking for Toby to give him a different job. Not finding him, he ordered me back to the shop to sign out a small jackhammer. For the rest of the shift, I lay inside a machine used to squeeze 3,000-degree billets into shape. This chore, intended for Toby, was the most hellish work I'd ever done. Wedged in a dark, cast-iron hole, I chiseled caked grease out of the machine's innards, striking metal against metal, a racket I thought could shake my skull right off my spine.

Enviable, I know. But Toby didn't know or care where I had gone, only that I'd left him with Emil and a ton of nasty waste. So now he wanted to poison me with whiskey. He left me with two choices: to stay and let him keep buying me shots until I was drooling on the bar, or leave as if he were driving me out, giving him a victory. It never occurred to me to decline his offerings, because the moment I waved one off, he would have shouted, "What? You too good to drink with me?" And our beef would move out to the blinding sidewalk, his friends following, and my friends—where the hell were they?—following me.

Fine, I thought, I'll take another shot from this prick. The first one hadn't even soothed me. I had grown more agitated as the summer went on and my bosses started telling me I could stay at Armco indefinitely. That would have made most guys happy, but letters kept coming from the registrar at Pitt asking about my plans for senior year, and, for the first time in my life, I was torn about my future. I had gone to college with a single goal: to become a lawyer, fight for justice, and make a decent living. But two years as an intern at a law firm had only convinced me that I had been carrying a romantic and unrealistic view of the profession. I faced three more years of school and a lifetime of chipping away at massive loans, arranging wills and mortgages. I was tired of being broke.

On his way to the toilet, Toby passed behind me and made a crack, but I didn't catch it. I sipped the rest of my beer and considered having another round, until I realized my friends were probably not joining me after all. Toby returned to his seat and prepared to order round three. He left me no choice.

At such times as this, I parted company with the braver men I knew growing up. I am part coward and part sensible. I'd seen blood and battle in schoolyards and bars, on sidewalks and in parking lots. One stupid remark led to another, then another. It was pointless and harrowing. If I had learned anything from seven years of Catholic school, it was to grant everyone a measure of respect, even those you'd rather spit on, especially those you'd rather spit on. My older brother could be a bully, as could his friends, and I got used to approaching them with calm self-assurance, speaking to them as if they were A-students, peers, and the tactic shocked and disarmed them. They felt respected while I made my point and escaped injury, or kept them from hurting someone else. I grabbed my beer and went to confront Toby. Out of the corner of my eye I saw the bartender backing toward the corner where she kept a Louisville Slugger.

"Thanks for the shots. What's the occasion?" I asked Toby.

"Fuck you. You wanna talk, let's go outside."

"Here's what I did last night," and I proceeded to describe the greasy sphincter where I spent the shift that he dodged by walking off to take a piss.

He laughed and threw a forearm into my chest, a love tap, then squared back to the bar and said to Carl, "Like I fuckin' care." I set my empty on the bar and waved to the bartender on my way out.

I crossed the brick street and turned around, just to be sure I hadn't been followed. Violence had erupted before on this spot. At Twenty-Third Street and Duss Avenue on October 4, 1933, a riot broke out at the end of a labor march that had started at the American Bridge works and continued for twenty blocks uptown, gathering more steelworkers as they snaked past National Electric. Organizers from all over the east coast, along with sympathetic journalists, amassed until they blocked the gates of what was then the Spang Chalfant plant—the same gates I had exited that morning on my way to Maxim's.

Wives of steelworkers joined them, carrying picket signs that protested the anti-union practices of the mill owners. The men, knowing they courted danger, carried sticks for protection against thugs routinely hired to disperse union uprisings in other places around Pittsburgh. The air rumbled with tension. The workers chanted and shouted, but fell into a hush when a carload of men in fedoras and dark suits parked on the curb across Duss Avenue. The men emerged bearing submachine guns. A few demonstrators met the armed men with upturned palms and calm questions. In the moments that followed, the crowd made way for a parade of more hired men, who wore armbands and carried a variety of weapons, from shotguns to clubs. They marched up the street to join the lead squad.

As I crossed the street back toward the gates, still uneasy from my standoff with Toby, I could have heard the shouts echoing through the decades. From the second floor of Maxim's, a newsreel photographer from the British agency Pathé opened the lens of his 35-millimeter movie camera and filmed the clash. An older man holding a twig at his side shuffled up to an enforcer cradling a Tommy gun and spoke to him in quiet tones. The gunman snatched the old man's stick and shoved him. "Hey! That ain't right!" a man in the mob cried out, and a scuffle erupted farther down Duss Avenue. Men shoved women who struggled to stay on their feet. Clubs flew above heads and shoulders and fell in crushing blows. The workers rushed from the gates to aid their comrades in the melée, and the armed men backpedaled into the middle of the street. The hired guns raised their rifles and fired. Shots, one right after another, exploded from gun barrels pointed toward the men at the gates. They ran. One man fell in a heap of dark wool. Others screamed and clutched bleeding wounds.

I stood in the safety of forty elapsed years on the sidewalk where laborers ran down the street and between buildings. They were not pursued. The shooters commandeered the gates while the other hired men tossed tear gas canisters at the fleeing demonstrators.

As the gas and smoke cleared, two of the men in fedoras checked the crumpled body, their fingers still poised on triggers. Later, another man hoisted the body over his shoulders and carried it away. That martyr was Adam Pietrowski. The names of the fourteen other marchers shot that day were not recorded.

In that spot and on that morning, the boilermakers in my bloodstream could have brought the scene straight into my sight. But I had never heard of the event. Now, thirty-some years after I crossed the street, the killed and wounded have been forgotten. Apart from my father's contemporaries, who were children at the time, locals know nothing of the skirmish. I learned from scant documentation that the only support the workers could count on came from activists who found support among socialists and communists, the few radicals willing to confront the owners of steel mills.

None of the outsiders were shot. They were intellectuals and dedicated social activists, who had come from the streets of Cambridge to the streets of Ambridge to take on the plight of workers. Among them: Jessie Lloyd Connor, a 1925 graduate of Smith College and granddaughter of Henry Demarest Lloyd, a journalist who fought Standard Oil and was a colleague of famed American communist John Reed. She escaped the violence and the gas, allegedly smuggling one of the main organizers out of town. But the local workers who lent nothing more than voices and who had little room to run, were pilloried. Grabbed on the run while gathering her skirts, Emma Brletic, a mother and the wife of a steelworker, was arrested, convicted, and sent to the Blawnox Workhouse for two years, a prison known as one of the worst in the world for what journalist Howard Fast called "the horror and degradation" visited upon political prisoners.

Coming out of the bar that morning, I felt disoriented, as if I'd been knocked off the course I had set for myself. Mistreated workers, my grandparents among them, fought for the safety and wages that made mill work tolerable. I was grateful, but could I stay and embrace the life? I saw how the union paychecks seduced restless men into the comforts and familiarity of home. That morning, instead of going to my car, I wanted to keep walking and find a new vantage point. I slipped back through the mill gates and headed for the river.

3

Rust and Restlessness

While working on the labor gang at Armco Steel, I had found a path snaking past the fuel tanks and leading to a bluff where I could catch a long view of the Ohio River. At night, I could hear clanging in the factories behind me and see roaring furnaces and glowing slag spilling down the riverbank. Two of my uncles worked beneath fire-breathing Bessemer converters on the right bank, making wrought iron under the protection of a union known as The Sons of Vulcan, and I could feel the breath of this god of fire and forge from where I stood.

Our lives were filled with discarded molten material—ash used for traction in the snow, nuggets of pig iron, sharp metal sheets, iron filings we gathered with magnets, mercury we kept as a treasured plaything, pipes welded together for the batting cage and plates walling our steel dugouts, corrugated sheets we learned to cut and bend into sleds and shields. Aluminum, steel, tin, and iron: scraps of it and lengths of it were lying around everywhere.

We collected it and threw it at each other, polished it and traded pieces of it. Like all boys, I was drawn to the way it rusted and flaked when I rubbed it, the way it rang against a ball-peen hammer, the way it smelled, sometimes pungent enough to make my fillings hurt.

I became intimate with wrought iron when I was fifteen, in the summer of 1970. Mr. Tierney, a teacher who had come from a family that owned furniture stores, bought one of the old houses in our neighborhood. Its white clapboards gave it a neat and stately look, augmented by lawns and gardens with countryside views behind it. The new houses, like ours, were brick tract houses without charm or character.

The acquisitive Tierney liked antiques, and soon after buying the house, he surrounded it on three sides with an ancient ornamental fence: two hundred yards of curly, rusty wrought iron in six-foot sections.

Kenny Fleeson, a joyful optimist with good manners and friendly parents, lived on the other side of my neighborhood. We had been pals since we were six, playing in pickup games of football, baseball, and basketball, covering every inch of the neighborhood on our bikes. Walking past Tierney's gloomy fence on our way home from junior high one day, we found it impressive but unsightly and, with all its flaking metal, untidy. We didn't like seeing rust. Metal could be strong and last forever if treated with respect and protected. Rust meant abandonment and surrender to the elements.

I had done some yard work, gutter-cleaning, and brush hauling for Tierney and knew he had money to spend on help. With no prospects of a summer job, we wondered if he might hire us to paint his fence. Emboldened by years of banging on doors, selling all matter of fundraising products—chocolates, raffle tickets, and cleaning agents—for our parochial school class and Boy Scouts, I convinced Kenny to come with me and present our idea to Tierney.

He asked us for an estimate, which took us by surprise. I thought he would offer me minimum wage, as he had done before. Local custom cast Tierney in the role of boss in such circumstances, and bosses told workers what they wanted and stated their terms. This guy treated us like adults, like contractors, and now I look back on this arrangement as the first in what would become a lifetime of freelance assignments. It also reminds me of how poor I have been at estimating my worth.

We paced off the fence and figured its length. Then we sought the advice of our fathers, who suggested we estimate only our labor and leave the purchase of materials up to Tierney. They gave us little help otherwise, because they, too, were unfamiliar with proposals and negotiations. In the end, we suggested three hundred dollars total, for wire-brushing the loose rust, priming, and painting.

Tierney bit his pudgy fist when he heard the quote. I did most of the talking, but I didn't really know what to say. I sheepishly explained that our estimate did not include paint and supplies, but that we would be careful not to waste paint, and we would clean up every day. We promised that we would remove all the rust. As a high school history teacher, he knew how to read us and showed his pleasure at our proposal. He also tried to remind us, even warn us, about the enormousness of the job. That's when I knew we had him hooked, and we assured him that we could do it.

Had I listened and showed more patience in responding, I might have picked up his incredulity and willingness to pay more. But I was in a hurry to shake his hand and get the negotiations over with. I don't remember his exact words in accepting our bid, I only recall that he asked me to repeat it, then looked at Kenny to be sure he agreed.

Suddenly we had a summer job, and we set to work every morning brushing and scraping the iron curlicues and filigrees, busting our knuckles and spitting flakes that flew into our mouths as well as our eyes, ears, and hair. Once we had peeled away the rust and burnished the metal to a tawny glow, we began to brush on the primer and saw that the pockmarked metal drank paint. Nooks and crannies, which we feared would immediately rust again if not filled, required that we slather paint with sodden brushes as it ran down our fingers and arms and splashed on our faces.

Preventing corrosion demanded that we use another heavy metal in the process. Only lead-based paint would do, which required that, at the end of every day, Kenny and I bathed our equipment and every inch of our exposed skin with turpentine. We soon learned that we could coat our skin with Vaseline every morning before we began, which would make the paint come off with less scrubbing.

I can still picture how sweat pushed through the petroleum jelly on my arms and hands on July afternoons, and the splatters of maroon primer we wore all over after only an hour of painting. Crawling on the grass to coat the low rungs, Kenny and I were embarrassed when pretty Peggy Miller, whom I loved at first sight and had kissed a hundred times behind tree houses and bleachers, on Ferris wheels and at basement make-out parties, straddled her bike and visited us while we worked on the sections by the road.

We got used to being a summer sideshow: two tall, skinny boys in paint-caked jeans and oily, spattered undershirts, our faces streaked with primer, Kenny's trim blond hair and my unruly afro jammed under cheap, disposable painters' caps. We could be seen every day by every neighbor, laboring at an endless task, objects of pity, often kneeling behind iron bars. The visitors and spectators, expressive in their sympathy and amazement, entertained us as we inched along, our transistor radio blaring Mungo Jerry: *...in the summertime, you got* *women, you got women, on your mind. ... If her daddy's rich take her out for a meal, if her daddy's poor just do what you feel.*

In the back forty, we scraped and painted through bushes and shrubs that grew along the fence, supplying an unforgettable memory of a mammoth forsythia that swallowed Kenny and shook with his struggling paint strokes. When Tierney went off with his family for a day trip or vacation, we slipped out of our workboots, and sneaked into the house, padding through the laundry room to the kitchen, where he kept a homemade appliance we had never seen before our first visit—a small refrigerator rigged to hold a keg of beer, with a tap sprouting from the top. We filled our thermos bottles with cold Iron City and stole back to the cool garage.

There, in the extra bay, sat a 1951 Ford that Tierney had picked up at auction, its windshield cracked and its paint worn and blistered with rust. We climbed into the front seat where the threadbare upholstery smelled of Pall Malls and my grandfather's closet. Carefully sipping our beers, we leaned back and dreamt aloud about buying the car and reconditioning it.

"He just bought it. He's not gonna sell it," I reasoned.

"Doesn't matter," Kenny said, "I don't think he works on cars."

"True. He might just let it sit here until we could afford it."

"I'd paint it black, add mags and slicks," Kenny said.

"Yeah, that'd be cool. But I think I'd take it right back to the original green, like it came off the line."

Palming the wheel, I leaned my head back, looked through the spidery cracks in the windshield, and saw us tearing down Route 66, laying tracks on the sand at Daytona, hugging the shoulders of Big Sur.

Every day I battled oxidation—ravages of the past. Being penned-in by that massive fence made me want to bust out, hit the road, go as far away as I could. All the way to the sea. From there I could learn to cross it, or sail along the coasts I knew from the maps I had pasted to the wall at my bedside— in and out of Maine's rocky harbors, the stretch of the Adriatic from Venice to Corfu, or, like an aimless pirate, through the Caribbean. Jacques Cousteau had introduced me to the sea, the Lone Ranger had made me want to go west, and James Bond opened the whole world to me. I cut out pictures, varied and without theme: Sherpas cooking in the Himalayas, Tupis poling up the Amazon, and preppies schussing down Vermont slopes. That wall held my dreams and idols. Henri Cartier-Bresson (whose name I never mentioned to anyone because I couldn't pronounce it) and his *Life* magazine photos allowed me to play in the streets of Spain. Some excursions were near at hand. W. Eugene Smith's studies made me ache to wander Pittsburgh with the Kodak Brownie I got for my first communion. When I had trouble sleeping, I concocted scenes that usually began with falling out of the sky or emerging from the woods into, say, the middle of a French village, where I notice a man washing his car and offer to finish the job, after which he invites me in to meet his family, have some bread and butter, the likes of which I had never tasted, and I slowly learn their culture. Arriving with nothing but my wits and cheerful nature appealed to me most, the anticipation of being forced to learn as I went along. In my fantasies, I dropped into more places that way, splashing into a fountain in Amsterdam, bouncing off the awnings above a bazaar in Tunisia, and *whump!* onto a Polynesian beach—all prompted by the photos on the wall.

By early August, the fence wore an impenetrable batter of paint, and we had learned a lesson in estimating our worth. We had worked for sixty-two cents per hour, less than half of minimum wage. Tierney paid us with three hundred one-dollar bills, counting each dollar out and stacking them before us. Now I could take off. I might have dreamed of Bali Ha'i, but I settled for Kokomo, Indiana. One of my favorite cousins lived there and I found a cheap student airfare that would take me to Indianapolis. I probably still smelled faintly of turpentine when I boarded the jet at the Pittsburgh airport and became the first person in my family to fly.

Now, thirty-seven years later, the fence has never seen another dab of paint. Tierney has long passed, the '51 Ford disappeared, and the house has changed hands several times. The fence still stands, a little blemished but in much better shape than when Kenny and I saw opportunity in its rust. Driving past the fence reminds us of two boys who learned how to honor a miscalculated commitment. As the owner of a small manufacturing outfit, Kenny's become an expert in solvents and resins, still stripping and coating. And I have come to see rust as a weathered narrative, blistered by time and neglect, shedding tales of Vulcan's men, calling upon the restless to apply a durable sheen.

4

Milk and Honey

My father, like most of his fellow veterans, couldn't wait to get home from Japan and never gave the slightest thought to leaving again. During the war, the federal government built a housing project for temporary steelworkers who came to build the war machine, near Legionville, where the first standing army of the United States was born. The duplexes of Anthony Wayne Terrace very much resemble a military base, and were sold to returning servicemen and their families.

Our apartment at The Terrace seemed perfect for my father, Milton (the only Milt in town), and my mother, Betty. She looked just like the brunette Betty in *The Flintstones*, which made her feel very American, even though she preferred Elizabeth, or Liz. "I can't imagine," she said, "Richard Burton marrying someone named Betty Taylor."

Five years younger than Milt, Betty had watched him grow into a man as she sat in the pews of Divine Redeemer Roman Catholic Church. Czechs, Slovaks, and Hungarians—a tiny minority, even among largely European neighbors—made up most of the congregation, led by a pastor who could speak their language.

Betty and Milt were both educated by the nuns at the Divine Redeemer primary school, but their families had only a passing acquaintance. They walked to separate high schools,

Milt to Ambridge, and Betty, who lived on the southern border of town, to nearby Leetsdale. In church, Betty, her sisters and parents, everyone in the congregation, noticed Milt, the tall, lanky sailor with the Jewish name when he reappeared in uniform after the war ended. On his arm was his fiancée, Elaine Marti, a Methodist girl of Italian and French heritage. She converted to Catholicism for him and they married in the wave of matrimony that followed the war and triggered the Baby Boom.

At the time, Betty, a former cheerleader and newspaper editor in high school, submitted to her father's view that boys should go to college and girls should become nurses or find a job and live at home until they were married. Every day she rode a streetcar into Pittsburgh where she eventually became a secretary for an executive at Bethlehem Steel. For a child with five siblings, raised in a house shared with two other immigrant families, she was living a dream, dating an older college boy, and traveling with friends to beaches and resorts.

The newly married Milt and Elaine moved into Anthony Wayne Terrace. Within a year, Elaine became pregnant. As a girl, she had contracted spinal meningitis that left her with damaged lungs, nothing that would stand in the way of a typical pregnancy or delivery. But a full twenty hours in labor proved too much for her.

"A nurse came down the hall and told me we had a son," recalled Milt. "I was thrilled, exhausted, and ready to celebrate. I had cigars. We'd already picked out a boy's name: Mark Allen. Then a doctor came out and gave me the bad news." Torn by the conflicting emotions of gaining a son and losing his wife, my father never told me the details until recently. He remembered the jacket he was wearing and the rosary he had been fingering in his pocket throughout his endless wait. "I remember nothing else, not who was with me, nothing. I went numb."

It was Easter Sunday, and the pastor announced Elaine's death in church. Upon hearing the news, my mother and the rest of the congregation gasped.

My father always spoke tenderly of Elaine and we counted her parents among our grandparents. "Afterwards," Betty recalled, "I'd see them in church on Sundays: your father, his parents, his sister, and the baby. It just broke my heart." A year or so later, she noticed that Milt had begun to regain his purposeful gait and his quick smile.

Milt noticed her too, a poised beauty with graceful manners and blue-green eyes that reminded him of the ocean around Hawaii where he had been stationed before setting off for Japan. "All of a sudden, one day, I saw that she was grown up and beautiful. I said to myself, 'I'm gonna marry that girl.'"

She must have liked his confidence. A year later, they were married, and my mother restored Milt's faith by surviving my birth. Mark and I shared a tiny room at the Terrace. Its rowhouses and duplexes each had lawns the size of four burial plots, as if we would all live out our lives there. The backyards swarmed with mothers, kids traipsing in and out, sitting on stairs, digging in dirt, splashing in inflatable pools, and wailing at the top of their lungs. Endless pots of coffee kept the mothers going, passing along wives' tales from each of their mothers' corners of the world. Marinara and meatballs became competitive. Some husbands came home at regular hours, others worked shifts, and the streets rarely fell silent. One man would be cracking open a beer after work while another brewed coffee and laid sandwiches in his lunchbox.

We lived in a duplex, two bedrooms upstairs, living room and kitchen downstairs. Because each family had purchased a share in the project, each cared for their properties and made improvements. Twenty years later, when Milt saw my cousin's new condominium, he stood in the parking lot and said "Oh, we used to call these *projects*."

My mother loved raising children. "I liked everything about it. I liked playing with you kids." Ignoring the breakfast dishes, she would rather sit on the floor with us, assemble Tinker Toys, and push trucks down the hallway. In all weather, she dragged us outdoors. While other mothers set their kids loose to play while they smoked and drank coffee, Betty kept playing, in sandboxes, leaf piles, and snowbanks.

Living near a large, extended family meant visiting, lots of visiting, and always visiting on Sundays. Without Sunday gatherings, they would have to rely on the phone to keep up with every detail of each other's lives and the immigrant elders met the phone with mixed emotions, given their suspicion of science—A voice coming over a wire? You're crazy—and they worried about privacy, having escaped nosy communists and dictators. If they had a phone, the line was shared by a party of strangers who could eavesdrop, and the phone's receiver was attached to an eighteen-inch cord. Clearly, the phone was useless for visiting.

After Sunday Mass, we dedicated the day to visiting the assortment of Eastern Europeans attached to my mother's family, the Rosols, most of whom were born in Czechoslovakia. She had three sisters and two brothers, and the Sunday gatherings included my grandmother Anna's contemporaries and elders: cousins, uncles, aunts, and friends, all of whom once shared a single house when they first arrived in Ambridge.

In their apartments and houses or out in their tiny gardens where I stood at eye level with the tomato plants, I felt a

European atmosphere coming through a profusion of lace my grandmother had tatted, old woodcuts, plates and prints with scenes of Carpathian peasants and landscapes, Bohemian pottery, and one particular statue of a lithe woman shading her eyes and looking out, as if she had seen a faraway figure, though her features withheld emotion or expectation. She made me sad as I connected her to the immigrants in the dining room, so far away from home. Every week my relatives celebrated having a haven where they had sunk new roots. Here was family, not every member through blood, but close enough. And more could be on their way. Doors opened readily when anyone showed up and visitors stayed as long as they liked. I still have relatives who would never think of staying in a hotel if kin live nearby, even if someone ends up sleeping in a barn.

I felt embraced at the heart of this world where children were seen as divine gifts. Our preciousness faded as we grew older, but until our voices changed, the toothless elders beamed as they adored me, my siblings, and my cousins.

We gathered at a number of small houses in Ambridge. Regardless of the address, the *whoosh* of the opening door issued a blast of moist cooking odors—yeast, tomatoes, cabbage, pork—cigarette and pipe tobacco, hairspray and sweat. In the forest of adult knees and shins, I located my cousins and unrelated children who we counted as cousins. We were sent into the back alley or a distant room to play. As a toddler, though, I preferred to slip away from the outdoor games and crawl under the broad dining room table, where I could be surrounded by the din of merrymaking and the music of adult voices.

I sometimes found another kid there, and we quietly ran trucks along the table's gate-legs, petted a dog, or stacked wooden blocks. Surrounding us were black and brown shoes, shined for Sunday but showing hard wear, brogues and new work boots on the men, thick-heeled pumps on the older women and flimsier heels for the young mothers. Betty kicked hers off. I recognized her toes.

From there, I could pantomime with my playmate while listening to the adults' voices, taking in the whole ensemble, sorting the tones, since their language made no literal sense to me. I relied on cadence, codas, like improvisational jazz, and the solos I could identify—Uncle Steve, the saxophone, Ucina a reedy clarinet, the percussion of my grandfather. I hear them now in the arrangements of Dave Brubeck.

Tones of urging and teasing came through, too, sarcasm and argument, a sudden laugh, the ring of shot glasses colliding in a toast followed by the silent quaff, and the clatter when they hit the table. Growls and sighs, all part of the Sunday afternoon jam. A crust of bread would fall under the hem of the homemade tablecloth, and I might feed it to the spaniel or eat it myself. I felt safe, obscured, and tenderly suffocated.

We were loved—by more than our parents, by everyone crammed into those houses, faces I can still see attached to names I can scarcely remember. Some were part Czech, Hungarian, Slovak, Ukrainian, Polish, and Croatian, but they had enough similarity in their language to understand each other. Most of them I'd seen earlier at Divine Redeemer, where masses and sermons were occasionally delivered in Slovak.

The languages and customs were so similar, the boundaries between those nations so mutable, that Betty had grown up as a proud Slovak with a chilly attitude toward Czechs, only to learn later she was, after all, Czech.

She once told me how deeply those who had emigrated missed relatives in the old country and how they cried for them. I remember my grandmother adhering to a daily schedule of prayers for those who had been left behind. On these Sundays, however, they spoke openly about the good fortune of being in America. The Second World War and the rise of the Soviet Union had convinced them of the volatility of their homelands. So they had little sentiment about the past, which became increasingly murky as they tried to forget it. They tied their identity to the present—where they worked, who they loved, their gardens, their trees, and vines. In an effort to protect the American-born children from their sorrows, they filtered their memories, leaving us only their food, their company, and the ability to understand commands in their language.

Three years before I was born my maternal grandfather, George Rosol, succumbed to the latent effects of mustard gas. I had thought of him as a hero, "jumping over bullets" as he had told others, and running from trench to trench in the First World War. Years later I figured out that the bullets were American, which meant my grandfather had fought for the "enemy."

Familial love went beyond sustaining me. During my high school years, when I hobbled to my grandmother Rosol's apartment after basketball practice, she knelt to cradle my swollen ankles, apply a poultice of grated potato, and wrap them in vinegar-soaked rags. Then she would cook dinner, standing at the stove, murmuring Our Fathers and Hail Marys as a device to time the food's readiness in her skillet. Some evenings she ate with me and other times she simply stood back with her feet spread and her speckled hands folded at her waist, watching me through watery blue eyes.

She read Slovak newspapers and magazines that carried stories she refused to tell me about, even when I asked, insisting that the stories were doctored by the communists and couldn't be trusted. Because I saw her often and knew her friends, I asked about her days and plans and she asked me about school and sports, scolding me for too much jumping and running.

Although our conversations ran shallow, our intimacy flourished in silence, in folding pastries together, in washing dishes, and trimming cabbage leaves. What our visits lacked in text was made up with texture. When dinner was over and dishes were clean, she filled a small enamel pot with milk and set it over a low flame. I watched the care she took with everything she touched, the grace with which she glided across the kitchen, fetching cups and saucers, while the sweet smell of scalded milk slowly rose, never escaping her attention. She moved everywhere as if in a meditation. Setting the cup before me, and one for herself, she filled them with the steaming milk.

She brought honey to the table and we spooned it into our cups. This sweet, simple cupful rose straight out of Exodus, a symbol of deliverance, a combination of earthly fertility and divinity that bathed my face. "It's good," she said with her first sip, then set the cup back in the saucer and smoothed the tablecloth around it, looked up at me, and smiled as if trying to tell me something. I waited.

"You come tomorrow," she said.

Then we carried our cups and saucers into the living room, also her bedroom, to watch *Gunsmoke*. If it wasn't on, I opened my homework while she read a newspaper for American Czechs and Slovaks. Though she'd married a peasant and gone to live in his village where his parents put her to work on their farm, she had been raised by intellectuals.

I first noticed her hands when I was four or five. We pulled weeds in her garden. I tore off the tops and tried to mimic her, the way the knuckle of her index finger pressed into the dirt before expertly extracting roots and all. Her hands happily entered soil, yet were pink and delicate while she tatted lace and cut noodles, dried my tears and pinched rosary beads.

My paternal grandparents were entirely different. Grandma Hertneky moved her small hands swiftly, to explain herself, to stroke a cheek, to knead, or slice, or chop, to crochet or deal a quick hand of rummy. She bit her nails, unlike her husband, who carefully trimmed his, perhaps compensating for two fingers that had been lopped off by machinery in the mill. The remaining digits were long and strong, and fluttered to reveal a heart too tender for his era—when a man's duty included wringing the necks of chickens. He would rather eat beans. And he knew the day would come when he could leave the killing to his sons.

Milt could understand most of the Sunday table chatter, but couldn't participate because his parents had spoken only English at home. His mother carried a kind of hillbilly patois adopted by immigrants in the mining and iron-smelting valleys south of Pittsburgh. Betraying her best efforts to shed Old Country ways, her ancestry imbued her with Gypsy superstitions: tossing salt over her shoulder, consulting cards, and reciting incantations that sounded more like witchcraft than the tiny prayers we were taught in Catholic school.

Her superstitions ran counter to Catholicism but she managed to invest her belief in both. She loved to play cards and bingo. Competition was fierce at church picnics every summer; when she would scooch over to make room for me to sit with her in an attempt to change her luck, she'd have me pick up a new hand, stack the cards together, and hand them to her, face down, just so. When the cards would start to come her way, she kissed me and hugged me, trying to keep me distracted from seeing my friends running by, throwing water balloons or waving streamers of crepe paper. She tugged at my shorts and kept me closer, buying me sodas and snacks, "You can play in a few minutes. I need your luck. You have very good luck," she'd say, pressing a few coins into my hand.

What could be better for a kid's self-esteem? But my grandmother didn't know that word and probably would have thought it had something to do with masturbation. The "charm" my grandmother saw in me she shared with my practical, yet superstitious grandfather, who may have had his doubts but took me fishing for the stated reason of bringing him luck. Granted, I interpreted all of this and may have exaggerated it. I know I *felt* lucky. One morning, while I stood on the stoop, waiting with my berry-picking bucket, I overheard my grandfather say "I don't know what we're gonna find for berries today." And my grandmother whispered back, "Oh, you'll find them. He has the luck."

Their messages were subtle and I don't know if they had imbued the sense of having good luck in their other grandchildren, but it made me feel like I had special powers, and I soon learned how to be careful with them. When I first saw my grandfather kiss a corpse at a funeral home, I asked my grandmother why he did that. "It's for luck. He wants him to rest in peace," she said. "You want me to do it?" I shot back. "I have the luck." And she slapped me. On my seven-year-old face. Hard, but not enough to make a scene. She squeezed my cheeks together, looked me straight in the eyes and said, "Don't you ever speak of your luck." Even now I worry as I write this.

Facing the open casket of someone he loved, Milt almost always kissed the corpse, a practice said to ward off visits from the deceased. Very few others did it. These touches of Romany set my father's family apart. In addition to his dark eyes and olive skin, my father's attitudes and behaviors matched those of Gypsies—he was tough, inventive, engaged, optimistic, and ready to dance and stay up late into the night, especially around a campfire. And his silliness and play belied a chilling darkness at his core and a talent for frightening both children and adults. A routine phone message from Milt carried a foreboding tone.

"Paul? Call me. Soon as you can."

What was I to make of that? Just about anything, from an aneurysm to an apple strudel recipe gone bad.

Some of the Gypsy blood came from my great-grandfather, a former miner and owner of a boarding house in the West Virginia coal fields, who hosted a Sunday dinner and card game after moving to Ambridge. Their triple-decker held three generations and every bed sagged under the weight of a crowd, but friends and neighbors piled in for feasting, games, and music. I know only legends of these gatherings—of the old patriarch trying to master flutes and concertinas that ultimately frustrated him. Witnesses say he often ended the musical portion of an evening by throwing the instrument high into the branches of an elm in the back lot.

In my early twenties, at a friend's wedding, I passed by a table where a tiny crone sat forward in her chair, tightened her grip on her cane with her left hand and snatched my cuff with her right. I bent down to hear her.

"Are you a Hertneky?" she asked.

"Yes, I'm Paul. Milton's son."

She told me her name, and then said, "I want to tell you about your great-grandfather. I've never told anyone this, about his blindness."

I had heard that the old man had gone blind before he died, yet still kept his place at the table, if only to drink and strangle a clarinet with the womenfolk doting on him. As the Sunday night card games wore on, the children from the neighborhood stretched out on the floor and slept until their parents came back for them in the morning. I pulled up a chair and faced the old woman while she composed herself, held my hand, and raised her rheumy eyes to the ceiling.

"Well, they all believed he stopped playing cards because he went blind," she said. "But I was one of the kids on the floor. After everyone left, I used to watch him, pretending I was asleep. He kept the light on, looked down at us, and carefully stepped between every one of us, never woke anybody up. Then he turned the light out. He did that for years."

When I told my father, he sighed, and then laughed. "I'm sure it's true. Sounds just like him, fooling people, keeping a big secret and a joke all to himself."

My grandfather, whom I would know for twenty years, did the same, taking satisfaction in secrets, white lies, gambling and stone-faced denial, helped by being a man of few words. Fewer than Paul Newman's Hud or Clint Eastwood's Josie Wales. In fact, he admired cowboys—one of his uncles had skipped past the coal mines and become a rancher in Colorado. Like their protagonists, he figured if he had to say more than two sentences, he hadn't thought about it long enough.

He wore one of two brown fedoras when he left the house, a slightly tattered, broken-in one with a hole in the crease where he pinched it to take it off, and a newer one for Saturday night and Sunday morning. Their wide brims shaded his eyes and elephantine ears set on a face craggier than the bark of an oak. Following a heart attack, my grandfather was told to quit smoking and my grandmother refused to give him money for cigarettes. So he shoplifted them by the carton and hid them all over his basement. I ran into him on the street once, mid-cigarette, and he held it behind his back, the smoke rising over his hat, chatting without taking a puff in front of me, as if granting me that respect might convince me to honor his secret. And it did.

After three years in The Terrace, while Betty was pregnant with her second son, Christopher, in 1958, my parents bought a single-family house. To reach it we had to pass through Legionville Hollow, where troops once trained to fight Indians on the frontier. The road climbed onto a ridge where, in the late 1950s, a fastidious German builder named Miller scratched out two looping roads and eventually built fifty houses with three basic designs. He built brick houses, made to last. My parents lived there for the rest of their lives, their contemporaries and old friends surrounding them. When they arrived, it was called the Miller Plan, or simply "The Plan." How charming to grow up in a neighborhood called The Plan, as if it were the only Plan in existence. The name conveyed a promise, a map to the future, and it stuck until Miller built a second plan. Then our neighborhood became Lynnwood Heights, but was still known as The Plan.

Miller built the houses as quickly as he could, to keep up with demand from returning servicemen and their growing families, who were happy to move in as soon as water ran from the taps. My father had felt cramped at The Terrace. At six feet four inches tall and active from the moment he stepped out of bed, the outdoorsman needed more elbow room than the housing project allowed.

The Plan amounted to thirty houses sitting on hillsides of dirt. To keep the terrain from washing away, the homeowners needed retaining walls that might hold any semblance of landscaping in place. They were men who tackled such projects themselves. Milt and Louie Colorito designed a cement block shaped like a home plate, and devised a mold to create it. Rudy Henger, who lived next door, joined the partnership to buy a small cement mixer. Soon, the men brought home bags of cement, and dump trucks came to drop mounds of sand and gravel on our driveway—a filthy thrill for the neighboring kids, who played all over the mounds with trucks and buckets, while our fathers shoveled sand, gravel, and dusty cement into the mixer and poured the blocks while drinking beer and smoking cigarettes.

They talked about their jobs. Milt and Louie worked as draftsmen for the American Bridge Company, producing detailed drawings for how beams and girders would be assembled for bridges and buildings. Rudy worked the production line at Armco Steel. A mostly silent and hard-working German, he had grown up on a farm about an hour north of Ambridge.

All three men were raised by immigrants, with different foods, different languages, and in separate ethnic neighborhoods. The war had confirmed their status as Americans, first and foremost, and our new neighborhood gave them far more room than the houses where they had grown up.

I liked hearing adults refer to the house as a "ranch," because it suited my image as a cowboy. I had several fantasy lives— cowboy, Cherokee, sailor, and frontiersman among them. I viewed our three-quarters of an acre and surrounding woods as an entire universe complete with sledding hills, streams, giant cherry trees, battlegrounds, and ballfields.

Babies were booming out of every house; playmates came in bunches. Mothers shooed their kids out of the house in the cold and snow as well as in the summer rain. Betty believed fresh air to be a cure-all, an agent of happiness, and salvation for herself. So she bundled us up in winter, stripped us down in summer, and sent us out to develop our social skills. She knew we had plenty of playmates. We roved in pairs, gangs, and solo, on bikes, in wagons, and on foot around the looping neighborhood, gathering in backyards, and wooded tracts.

We scavenged in streams for salamanders and crayfish, and diverted the water into pools, lining sluiceways with flat rocks and rusted lengths of angle iron, trying to encourage a torrent. Civil engineers we were, in muddy bosks that felt like lost worlds to us. I often stole into the woods alone to enjoy solace, the silence, the rare thrill of doing things my way instead of the group's way, and to indulge my imagination.

My father's parents visited us nearly every night after dinner, even though they had already seen Milt at lunchtime. He packed his own lunch but went to their house in Ambridge to catch up on the thirteen hours that had elapsed since seeing them the night before. My mother tried to accept this craziness, but she stewed and rankled at my grandmother's nosy questions about how she seasoned the pork chops and why she used liquid laundry detergent when powder was clearly better.

Custom dictated that guests stay as long as they liked. You might think my grandparents had worn out their guest status, but Grandma Hertneky tucked us into bed most nights. Sitting on the edge of our beds, she told the only stories I would hear about the Old Country, not personal accounts, but folktales passed down from relatives who lived in and around Transylvania, which became a very real place to us—the reputed home of Frankenstein and Dracula! In her bedtime stories, ghouls roamed the woods and children went missing. When we pulled the covers over our heads, she caught herself, and tried to ward off the nightmares with tickling and vigorous back rubs, always finishing with a sharp whack on the buttocks to expel any lingering demons—a bit of magic that seldom worked.

5

Where Stories Went to Die

Because I was born an American, and for reasons I still guess at, my older relatives avoided telling stories about their lives in the Old Country. Save for gossip (which I now hold as the vernacular of my narrative past) neither of my parents conveyed tales, perhaps because they were too young to have developed a perspective on bygone events and felt little nostalgia. They also had only a passing, textbook knowledge of history, despite being surrounded by storied artifacts.

Betty and Milt often took us back to Anthony Wayne Terrace to visit the friends we made while living there. Among them were Dolly and Ernie Miketa, and their sons Dennis and Gary, who were roughly the same age as my brother Mark and me. Both of the boys were fun and energetic, but Gary seemed to have a sixth sense or at least a highly developed awareness that made him an extraordinary hunter, the kind of hunter who sees, hears, and shoots on target before others get their guns to their shoulders. When we were young boys, I would watch in amazement, crouching on a slag pile as Gary would paw at the soil for arrowheads. We found some, but he found many.

We could walk from The Terrace to the site of Logstown, a former Indian settlement along the Ohio. Half of the site was a scrubby field high above the river from which we could see a long way in both directions. A stream cut through the plateau that had been choked and gouged out by back hoes, making it look like a strip mine into which A. M. Byers, an iron smelting factory on the other end of what had been Logstown, dumped slag and waste. Today, the site would attract teams of archaeologists, but such opportunities are long gone.

Back in the early 1700s, several Indian tribes, seeking refuge from European invaders, established a trading center that became known as Logstown because it rose from an eddy along the Ohio where fallen timber had piled itself against the banks and supplied ready material for building longhouses and other kinds of shelter.

Just a day's walk downstream from where the Allegheny and Monongahela rivers meet at present-day Pittsburgh, Logstown attracted French and English military leaders and land speculators. Virginia's plantation owners, looking to expand their holdings in the mid-1700s, sent a twenty-one-year-old George Washington into the territory to make treaties with the Indians there and warn the French to stay away.

The venture nearly ended Washington's life, as a would-be assassin hired by French commanders took a close-range potshot at him and his guide. He returned to Logstown several times to cement his relationship with Chief Tanaghrisson, who would ultimately stand alongside Washington as they interrogated a wounded French military officer in the forests south of Fort Duquesne. In a fit of rage and vengeance, as Joseph Coulon de Jumonville knelt before him and Washington, Tanaghrisson drove an ax through the diplomat's head—a single blow that ignited the Seven Years War, the world's first global conflict, fought in America as the French and Indian War.

Later, the American Revolution kept the colonists busy,

and Indians along the western frontier enjoyed a respite from the flood of white men, a period of relative peace and prosperity. But soon after Washington became president, the scattered forces along the frontier found the Indians unwilling to give up their land and ready to fight to keep from being pushed west.

The president remembered Logstown, and its vantage point along the Ohio, and dispatched one of his most fierce, loyal, and reasonably sober generals from the wars against the Crown. At a crucial moment in the Revolution, when Washington asked him to lead special forces to attack the heavily fortified British stronghold at Stony Point, New York, "Mad" Anthony Wayne resolutely replied, "Issue the orders sir, and I will storm hell."

General Wayne hand-picked a force hanging around Pittsburgh after the Whiskey Rebellion and set up Legionville as a training camp for Indian fighters. With the help of the English and French ensconced around the Great Lakes, Native Americans tried to hold their ground against waves of new colonists, and terrorized the frontier. Responding to the bloodshed, Washington sent Wayne to defeat the Indians and, in doing so, established the nation's first army, the Legion of the United States, outfitted with leather-collared uniforms to protect them against harsh winter winds blowing up the Ohio River. Those uniforms were handed down in 1798 to the Marine Corps—eventually known as "leathernecks." Among the trainees at Legionville were future president William Henry Harrison, William Eaton who would lead the Marines into Tripoli, West Point founder Henry Burbek, Zebulon Pike, William Clark, and Meriwether Lewis.

We kids of the 1950s blithely played cowboys and Indians there, our pockets filled with three-hundred-year-old artifacts, splashing through mucky, polluted Legionville Creek—which

Washington described in his notes as "a swift watercourse" gushing from the escarpment below Logstown. We found only a trickle, seeping around mounds of ironmaking waste. But we also found musket balls, horseshoes, boot buckles, and arrowheads.

In school we never heard the stories of Logstown, its prominent visitors, its world-changing chief Tanaghrisson. Even though many of us passed the site every day, and Anthony Wayne's name was co-opted by everything from taverns to muffler shops, we learned nothing about the future president and most famous western explorers who fired those balls and rode those horses.

It was as though our recently immigrated teachers, parents, and grandparents had found virgin territory. Something had existed here before them, but it wasn't part of their story, so they looked past it, beyond it, really, into the future they saw waiting for them in the land of opportunity. The remains of Economy, another world-renowned and historically significant settlement in our midst, received the same shrug of indifference.

Teachers made "manifest destiny" sound noble. Righteous authority entitled every fortune seeker and prophet, from kings to Carnegie to a Hungarian coal miner advancing straight through mountains in a parade of acquisition. Exploitation? The word never came up, but every corner of Ambridge bears its stains.

I love this landscape, this amalgamation of cultures, but it all seems to have been done in haste, with no regard for what came before, probably because nobody talked or wrote about what came before. Would the fiery A. M. Byers plant have been built right there? Would life have been different if we had known the stories?

From the time I was a toddler, my father slowed the car as we passed Byers' twin Bessemer converters that were open to Duss Avenue. I would stand on the back seat and watch the giant thermos-shaped smelters tip skyward and shoot flames, sparks, and gobs of molten iron into the night air. Thirty feet tall and girded with heavy iron, these twin behemoths exhaled a sulfurous cloud that bathed the Ford in a warm wave, like standing in front of Godzilla when he's really pissed off. And I saw that show and felt that breath every week. Awesome. It ignited something in me that still burns.

The Byers iron mill opened in 1930, directly atop the remains of Logstown. I can only assume that the Daughters of the American Revolution found the sale and placement to be an affront, because, soon after the mill opened, the DAR erected a fifteen-ton granite boulder on the site, with a plaque that describes Logstown's history, concluding wistfully: "The importance of these events belongs wholly to the past."

That statement captured local understanding of history—not only American history, but our family histories. New immigrants resisted or downright refused to talk about their lives before they crossed the Atlantic. If important events on this stretch of land were thrown into the dumpster of the past, how significant could a foreign homeland or family be? Why bother telling stories, or seeking them out? But I couldn't help it. My curiosity felt like a constantly full bladder. I had to ask.

"I don't like to talk about the Old Country," my grandmother said, in broken English. The very word "communist" rattled her.

"What were the communists like?"

"They were men."

"Oh, please, Grandma, you gotta give me more than that."

"I *gotta* give you nothing," she said, making fun of my slang. "You want *kolachi*? I get some."

Boom. Interview over. Her immediate family back home had become victims of thug-style violence, confiscation, extortion, and became refugees. She could find no way to help them other than through her daily prayers. I thought she didn't want to tell her stories, when, I now understand, they were too hard to tell. She withheld her stories about moving from her urbane parents' home in the city to her new husband's peasant village, and leaving her family behind—then moving all the way to America—not because those events belonged to the past but because they festered in her still. They were too important to recount, and she was afraid of how they would end.

My most palpable sense of the Old Country came from an embroidered *perrina*, a down quilt that, by its smell and feel, conveyed details of the past, which my grandmother kept, locked in a cedar chest. Every family, social, and religious ritual carried a tradition but the roots of that tradition fell behind a veil stitched tightly by the crossing of steamer ships filled with hopefuls who were trying to forget the past and knew nothing of their future.

Frustration with my grandmother didn't faze my nosiness. I pleaded with the old folks to tell me about coming to America, and when they did, they worked their jaws and rubbed their hands, as if trying to wring out a way to put it. "It's good now. I work. I know machines. I grow food. I can dig. I can work all day. I'm strong." That's all they gave me, a Zen-like litany of their days—the skills that would allow them to stay, looking ahead, trying to forget the poverty, oppression, war, and corruption in Europe.

Surrounded as I was by silent immigrants and exploited landscape, I knew nothing of how this place, its people and resources, had made a difference in America. The stories never got out. Writers and artists have rarely emerged from the ranks of steelworkers. We left our portrayal up to outsiders, observers, photographers from the Works Progress Administration, industrial and union newsreel shooters, journalists from national newspapers who coined descriptions of Pittsburgh as "hell with the lid off." Every depiction, from the mythical steelworker Joe Magarac, to *The Deerhunter*, is shot through the same lens, portraying blue-collar stereotypes with detached, sympathetic reverence, usually in as simple terms as possible. Novelists and filmmakers came to working -class towns like Ambridge looking for characters, but, with few exceptions, twisted them into caricatures.

Today in Ambridge, locals are only too willing to tell their stories: steel and its attendant industries crashed in the 1980s. Ambridge, Youngstown, Akron, Toledo, Allentown, and hundreds more places like them now fall into the sad category of predecessors like Lowell and Waterbury, Worcester and Fall River, places that went down a long time ago and still haven't come back.

Several times every week for the first twenty years of my life, I watched those enthralling Byers' furnaces send flames into the night as they converted iron into steel with extreme heat, driving out carbon and "impurities"—ancient remains within the ores—and blasting them into dark clouds of smoky particles. We now know that the smoke did not simply ascend into heaven; it settled in our lungs, our hair and eyes, our backyards and our children.

Events never belong wholly to the past. Stories and human experience, like the earth's hardened elements, impurities included, can be dismissed, ignored, annealed with suffering and buried, but wherever we go, we carry them within us.

6

The Front Pew

Before starting primary school, I seldom left my neighborhood until Sunday morning, when my father drove our family along the ridge that hovers above the Ohio Valley and then plunges into the section of Ambridge settled by its first European immigrants.

As a little boy standing on the padded kneeler in the front pew of Divine Redeemer, I gazed at the stained glass windows, imagining their circles and panes as sour balls and lollipops, baseballs and footballs. Incense found my little nose and the scent has stayed there throughout my life. The choir and the reedy tones of the organ, sounding similar to the organ at baseball games, spilled from the loft, seducing me and arresting my attention.

Every Sunday, my parents marched their brood—Mark, myself, Chris, three years younger than me, and Laurie, only a year younger than Chris (our youngest sister, Maria, would arrive on my twelfth birthday)—into that front pew, left empty by bashful worshippers. From there we were obliged to pay attention to the ritual that unfolded. We behaved better, knelt straighter, and had a close-up view of the proceedings. Everyone witnessed when we fussed or involuntarily slugged each other.

Dressed in my Sunday best, I played with the tiny envelope

that held a dime, waiting for the usher to come with his long-handled basket so I could drop it in. That dime could have bought two fistfuls of bubble gum, but it never belonged to me, it belonged to the act of charity, to the simple motion of giving. I don't remember how I understood it, exactly, only that it would be done, just as I shined my shoes the night before and pressed down my multiple cowlicks in the mirror that morning. Those acts made me part of the ritual, part of the congregation, part of something bigger than myself.

And yet, I couldn't take my mind off myself. I thought about how I looked, how I comported myself. I compared my posture, my piety, my tie, my shoes and jacket, to those of other boys my age. I cared more about standing out than fitting in. None of that mattered to Mark, who knew a poke in the ribs could crack my façade. But because there would be hell to pay for bad behavior, things seldom got out of hand, and I could continue polishing my image.

Year after year in that front pew, face to face with Saint Joseph—the surrogate father of Jesus who seemed incomparably kind—standing there in varnished oak, a lily sprouting from his staff, I grew into a young man whose dimes increased to quarters. The parade of communicants passed just in front of us, and I cataloged the scent of their perfumes and aftershaves, liniments, tobacco, wet wool, and mothballs. As each one choked down a wafer, I studied their walks: the way they shuffled or shambled, clicked by on high heels, some shy and bowed, some sashaying, strutting, or marching, fresh out of the armed forces. My eyes followed friendly mothers, then pretty girls who grew taller and fuller, passing as if in one continuous procession that ran for eight straight years. I pretended to be praying or singing but devoted all of my attention to watching until I passed from fascinated to intoxicated, ogling by the age of twelve.

I had a different perspective during the week. The bus dropped off students of Divine Redeemer's primary school in front of the church every morning, and we took seats with our classmates for Mass. I recall deep and endless boredom, especially when the Mass was said in Latin, and how standing, kneeling, sitting, and singing, all done by rote, helped to keep me awake. How long could I lose myself in imagination or a flat-out trance, every bleeding day?

I prayed intently for something to happen. I begged God for an incident, and anything would do. Mostly, I envisioned chaos erupting and finding a way to help out. I imagined elaborate action scenes in which gun-wielding bad guys charged in, took us hostage, and desecrated the church. But I would sneak out, cut off the power, call the cops, create a distraction, outwit them, and have them begging for mercy by the time the police arrived.

All those masses drove me into one of two intense mental states—an interior circus whirling behind my eye sockets, or a relentless cataloguing of details that surrounded me. At times I'd seize upon odors, or coughs, squeaks, and individual voices, or I'd take note of loose or unmatched buttons, birthmarks and odd patches of hair, keeping track of who hunched or leaned back, who muttered or snored. Exaggerating their weaknesses made me feel strong and superior, allowed me to pity them and dream up more ways to save and protect them.

I saw congregants as sheep, an image confirmed by the gospels, and saw myself as a shepherd, just like Christ, whose behavior was held up as a model. "Remain humble," I told myself, but I felt like I belonged in that pantheon of haloed men depicted on the painting behind the altar. Looking around, I knew I belonged in the pulpit. Like a daily drug habit, all these masses injected pure delusion into my ego. I became a savior, a hero-in-waiting.

During the thousands of weekday masses we escaped without a sermon but on Sundays, we heard the analytical and oratory skills of Franciscan missionaries, some of whom shook me out of my monumental self-importance. Hearing these educated, well-traveled, passionate men take on philosophy, history, morality, poverty, belief, and the word of God, as they heard it, swept me up.

It made sense to me that priests were men like our fathers, who, without children, could spend most of their time reading, thinking, and caring for people. I treated them with reverence and was a good altar boy, in deference to their position in the community and out of respect for the life they led. They often laughed and joked. I felt comfortable with them. I encountered no monsters among them, and am grateful for my good luck, because their power met little resistance. I esteemed their education, articulateness, spirit, and embrace of poverty. I remember thinking: "what a great way to live," moving among the sick and poor, housing provided, volunteers to help, all those attentive listeners on Sundays. No money, but a complete wardrobe, a housekeeper, and tickets to ballgames from parishioners. A free education. Maybe a trip now and then. Retreats—I liked the way that sounded. And nearly as much of a chance of being a hero as a fireman or a cop. Celibacy? I wasn't sure what that meant, but it seemed doable.

I also liked the idea of being called to a vocation. It skirted the tricky notion of ambition, setting the chosen ones on a road prescribed by God, one without doubt, all-consuming and commanded by the heart. Ambition could make you forget where you came from.

For an honest workingman any work was a gift. "You workin'

good?" was the first question adults asked when catching up with a friend. While I heard plenty about jobs being earned and won, I came away with the impression that jobs were granted for being in the right place at the right time, for knowing a key person, for coming from a good family. Patronage played an important role in success. As such, ambition involved working a system and finding your place rather than lofty individual pursuits that fed only pipe dreams and led to disappointment, or worse, an air of superiority.

We were taught to get good grades, be kind and courteous, sing sweetly but harmoniously in the choir, humbly recite altar-boy Latin, play football and baseball as a teammate, make our parents proud. That would be ambition enough.

But all of that fell short of my heroic quest. Nuns and priests impressed me, and I watched their every move, studied their gestures and their manner of speaking. I noticed the way the nuns maintained composure and dignity in the name of service, whether teaching a stammering pupil or cleaning up a pool of puke.

As for the priests, they were performers on center stage, decked out in the most magnificent brocades and silks, one layer on top of another in colors that carried meaning for the occasion and the season. I admired the priests who struck a balance between drama and humility, who threw themselves into their performance in the purest effort to draw me in. They were doing it for *me*.

Wondering if I could bring the ceremony back to life on my own, I slipped a wine glass out of the kitchen cabinet and fashioned a square of cardboard and a handkerchief to serve as estimations of the Eucharistic tools. I cleared my dresser and laid out a fresh white cloth, cut circles out of white bread and mashed them into wafers, threw a bedsheet over my shoulders and, with or without the congregation of my siblings, did my best to transform Welch's grape juice and Braun's bread into the body and blood of Christ. Why not?

I was only playing of course. The dressing up, the melodramatic reading of Latin passages, pious intonations, exaggerated choreography, and scolding from the pulpit—I called it play. Yet I was dead serious about commanding attention and positioning myself to inspire, and to be touched by a hand from heaven. I yearned to transcend ordinary existence, to pray my way into enlightenment or to hear what the nuns referred to as "the calling."

All parents dream of grandchildren, but Catholic parents seldom dared to even speak the dream of having a son become a priest. Soon, I found an entire Mass-playing kit under the Christmas tree, complete with white plastic vestments with bold red crosses. I liked the bedsheets better, but I was thrilled to have all the props I needed for a suitable production. That's when my brothers and sister became a willing congregation. Santa had brought Chris a toy dashboard with a steering wheel, gauges, windshield wipers, and a horn he set on the kitchen table. Arranging chairs beside and behind him, he drove Mark and Laurie to Mass on our imaginary Sunday mornings.

After the real thing on Sundays, though, I had questions. I heard dogma that didn't make sense to me, and I couldn't wait for the ride home. Usually I seized upon liturgical inconsistencies—if God is all-forgiving, why Hell?—that sort of thing.

"Oh, no. Here we go again," Mark would groan, walloping me with his prayer book.

Betty would say, "It's okay. If you don't understand something you have to ask."

How hard could my questions be? I was only nine years

old. My parents had sixteen years of Catholic school between them and knew their catechism, but I interrogated them, week after week, well into my teens. When my skepticism veered toward blasphemy, Milt fell silent. I could see his jaws tensing. An exasperated Betty resorted to advice that I pray for faith and accept mysteries. They punished us for misbehavior in church, but never for questioning and doubt.

Betty and Milt listened as we presented our case, and asked questions before issuing orders, laying down the law, or punishing us. Perhaps because they both felt pressure to meet their own parents' expectations, they explained the hard-line argument, but once they got going they spoke in rebellious terms about issues like excommunication as punishment for divorce, giving me a sense that they recognized the tension between obedience and independent thinking, between sin and reasonable fun. Milt, as an elected leader in our church, would later defy the hierarchy and go toe-to-toe with the bishop of Pittsburgh over an edict to close Divine Redeemer. They fought for seven years. My parents showed open-mindedness and an eye for hypocrisy and inconsistency. Betty, for instance, liked gambling, slot machines, playing numbers with bookies (which Milt refused to enable out of reasons more mathematical than moral), and she teased church folk who scoffed at gambling then sold raffle tickets at church functions.

Betty expected her three sons to know how to cook and clean, and Milt often strapped on an apron, no matter how flowery or frilly. He pitched in with kitchen work, which was rare for men in his era. But Milt never concerned himself with being seen as anything less than a real man, making him easy to emulate.

When the smell of burning leaves mixed with the scent of solvent Milt used to clean his shotgun, we anticipated hunting season, even before we were old enough to join him. On a few Saturday mornings, while it was still dark outside, I'd feel my dad wiggle my big toe to wake me and order my brothers to saddle up for a trip to Latrobe, where my aunt's parents lived, in the heart of coal mining country. Milt picked up his parents along the way and we set out into the rising sun. At some point he would ask, "Did you hear that?" "No, what?" we would say, lifting our heads out of a sleepy fog. "That was the crack of dawn," he'd say.

Milt, his brother, John, a couple of local guys, and my aunt's brother Richard, a priest and professor at nearby St. Vincent's College, greeted each other, strapped on their field jackets, inspected their shotguns, and hustled out into the fields and woods. We joined cousins for a day of playing and chasing and leaping from the hayloft. Once the shadows lengthened and the steam of chicken stew and dumplings rolled into every room, we could hear car doors slamming and all three dogs barking. In the failing light, the hunters laid out their quarry on a tailgate: majestic ring-necked pheasants, perhaps a few ruffed grouse, and a fluffy row of rabbits. All had been field dressed. That is, gutted and stuffed with grass. We kids looked on admiringly as the men popped open pony bottles of Rolling Rock straight from the icebox. (These old-timers lacked a real refrigerator.)

Twelve adults and six kids wasted no time getting to the dinner table. And, after dinner, my brothers and I clambered down the basement stairs, into a humus-smelling cellar dominated by the coal furnace. Black duct pipes sprouted out of the top of the massive cast iron orb, a warm glow beaming through slits in the oven's door. We sat on a bench in the shadow of a single light bulb, leaning against the cool walls of stacked shale. Beside a washtub, my father worked deftly with a razor, first cutting off the cottony tail of a rabbit and reaching toward us with the gift. I had to pick it off his sticky, bloody hand. He used his knife to lop off the back legs at the knee. These, too, we collected, since nothing brought better luck than a rabbit's foot. Then he peeled away the skin, revealing the muscle and sinew, and inspected the carcass for buckshot, which he flicked out with the tip of his knife.

While he finished skinning all the rabbits, my brothers and I stroked our new feet and blew tails into the air. Then my father draped a skin over each hand and shoved his index fingers up into the still-attached heads. He concocted dialogue, spoken in a small voice, between the two puppets, who gestured and nodded and regarded each other and us with glossy black eyes. We giggled and listened to their story, holding their severed feet, their blood dripping down my father's forearms.

Like the priests during Mass, Milt transformed death into life, an imagined life, one in which a boy's aspirations of heroism could come true.

7

Sanctuary

The sidewalks of Ambridge in the 1960s were jammed with pedestrians running their weekend errands. And, on most evenings, Merchant Street, lined with shops, bars, and restaurants, gleaming with shiny cars and neon signs, drew families that walked arm in arm as they might in Naples or Athens. Clusters of clean-cut men stood on corners, smoking and waving to their friends, teasing or belting a few bars of "O Sole Mio" for the women leaning out of third-floor windows.

We spilled into public out of necessity. Families were growing faster than company housing could accommodate, with three generations occupying tiny apartments and houses built with full knowledge that immigrants demanded little in the way of personal space. These houses still stand, and are about the size of today's utility sheds.

In my family's house, we did homework at the kitchen table with my mother ironing behind us. When the session broke up, if I wanted to read I retreated to the basement, amid the laundry, casks of fermenting wine, and crocks of sauerkraut, my father running a jigsaw and listening to a ballgame on the radio.

The togetherness sometimes overwhelmed me and I sought out solitary havens—the woods or the cool order of an empty church. My favorite sanctuary was the most richly endowed and widely ignored building in town.

As I climbed its granite stairs, I passed under tall bronze lanterns that told me the Laughlin Memorial Library occupied a higher plane than the street out front. Thousands of steelworkers, six times a day, marched past the library and onto the bridge to Aliquippa. As they crossed, they surveyed their destination on the bank ahead, a continuous massive building that stretched for six miles downriver, the Jones & Laughlin steel mill—J&L to locals—a hulking, fire-breathing monster, bound by railroad tracks to the riverbank.

I rarely saw a mill worker stop at the library, or hang out there before or after work. They headed home, but not before filing into the back door of the saloon at the end of the block. Inside ran a long bar with no stools. The string of workers threw back shots of whiskey and beer chasers, then, like hot billets traveling down the rolling mill, exited the front door on the corner, where their wives picked them up, efficiently juiced to face domestic life in close quarters.

The library rose above the herd. In addition to its elevation, its brass doors demanded that a skinny twelve-year-old had to plant his back foot to pull them open. "There must be something really good in here, something important, like a treasure," I thought. When I entered, another world opened before me, as if I had been transported far away and into a refreshing, invigorating, and oddly familiar dimension in time. Apart from the matron at the front desk, who greeted me with a pressed smile and a nod, I was often completely alone.

Alexander Laughlin, no relation to the owners of J&L, built the library in memory of his son, who had served heroically in the First World War only to return home to die in a dentist's chair. Laughlin, an Ambridge industrialist and owner of Central Tube Company, took his cue from Andrew Carnegie, sparing no expense in building this public temple of erudition, right up to the vaulted ceilings, cherry tables, shelves, cabinets, Italian marble floors and columns, leather chairs, and an endowment that has kept it in sweet condition.

I took my pick of seats and views. Near the windows, sunlight warmed me. Facing the corners, I fell back into a wing chair and lost the world behind me. My family's house, the Catholic school and church, our neighborhood and the houses of relatives, all made me feel at home and part of a community, but the library made me feel whole, as if I could explore every corner of my own universe and the places I had never seen. The populace of books and the millions of ideas they contained set loose my dreams.

Drowsiness never threatened my quest. Instead, something I read while doing my homework had formed a question that nagged me, and I knew it could be answered by peeking in the reference section. The flat metal drawers of the card catalog spoke to me, promising entire volumes on the migratory fish of the Mississippi delta or the first closed sewage system. How could I resist?

I liked the way every step sounded important against the marble floors as I imagined myself pursuing knowledge and culture. In reality, I was simply scratching an itch, one after another. Chasing leads, I piled up fat books until I found one to take back to the table for closer inspection only to get waylaid in biography, following a thread from encyclopedia to compendium. Like a miser poring over his ledgers or an archaeologist on his knees with his brushes, I never noticed the hours rushing by on a current of curiosity.

During hot summer days at home, my friends and siblings grumbled until one of the mothers took them to the Ambridge pool, a massive cement playground of chest-high water.

Mayhem ruled, pitched with peer pressure and wet, snotty, kid-on-kid cruelty. I was afraid of the water and wore a bathing suit the way a Chihuahua wears a tutu, so I begged to be left at home or taken to the library. In winter, movies offered escape from the busy house and family, but the library allowed me to direct and star in my own movie—a mad chase, streaked with impressions, foreignness, and startling facts.

Left undisturbed among maps and magazines, I investigated far-flung nations, their mountains, shores, and people, their dwellings, their towns, leaders, legends, and heroes. Connecting the word "culture" to the mold growing in Petrie dishes in science class, I slipped my reading about places under a sort of microscope and found the languages, arts, innovations, and literature feeding off the surroundings, climate, and history. New smells seeped out of the pages of Conrad, new fears out of the caves of Twain, and I swam in all of it without bearings or sense of time.

Noticing the sunbeams had slipped from the table and climbed the walls, I resurfaced with the feeling of having been swimming undersea or through a passageway between worlds—I remember it as if it were yesterday because it still happens. I feel woozy, shaking off a familiar disorientation, wiping my palms down the length of my torso as if some slime remained from a membrane through which I passed. How long had I been away?

Novels were best for borrowing, so I went to the desk and checked them out. Finally, I savored one last exhilaration— walking away from the mess I left behind. The librarians insisted on restacking every book, so I felt like a rock star leaving a trashed hotel room.

Out on the sidewalk, nobody asked me what I had been doing there. I held my affection for the library privately, because what I did there felt illicit and indulgent. I could pretend there, to be purposeful and scholarly; the librarians probably giggled. The act came easily, though, captivated as I was by the excursions, stories, facts, no-shits and ahas. I wanted to do it forever. As far as I could tell, the hours I spent in the library led to nowhere in particular, no purpose—an admission that made me feel guilty, because every educated person I had met had become useful: accountants, lawyers, nurses, doctors, and teachers. Me? I was just feeding my fascination.

I hustled off to the Tick-Tock Dairy, a soda fountain, where I could call for a ride home and watch the workers get off the shuttle bus that carried them across the bridge from J&L. Their hair shone and their faces still glowed from the showers. They wore clean clothes and carried empty lunch buckets. Watching them, I pictured myself among them, one of the guys, joking, prosperous, and woven into the community. But as soon as I looked back into my milkshake, I dreamt of other places or another kind of life. I noticed the owner of the Tick-Tock, drying his hands on his apron while standing at the front window, waiting for the guys to come in and buy cigarettes. He had found a way to live and work outside of the mills and I admired him. Yet, I figured a time might come when I would join the boys outside.

8

The Nation's First Economy

In 2005, I pulled the Laughlin Memorial Library's brass doors open and noticed green stains on the limestone pedestals where the bronze lampposts once stood before they were dragged away by vandals for the price of salvage. The stains ran like tears for what Ambridge had become, a desperate place where desecration was the least of crimes.

Late in the afternoon, as I descended the stairs, my youngest sister, Maria, passed on her way home from work as a counselor in a high school across the river. On my twelfth birthday, an otherwise routine Tuesday, I found my hugely pregnant mother putting the finishing touches on my favorite dish—melt-in-your-mouth breaded pork chops. Betty wasn't about to let a few labor pains stand in the way of making me happy. Mark and I ate dinner early and left for a Boy Scout meeting. Four hours later, my parents called from the hospital to say Maria had been born. From that day on, we've had a special bond.

I asked Maria to park and walk onto the bridge with me. She zipped up her jacket in the face of a chilly autumn wind. The massive J&L Steel mill across the river had been demolished, leaving a barren stretch of flat sand along the Aliquippa banks. You might think enterprising landowners would capitalize on the assets of riverfront real estate—beautiful views, long walks, land enough for a golf course, a water park, a marina or a residential village. But, instead, a new cement and plasterboard plant had taken root, an Escher-like complex of tipples and conveyors. Worse, county officials planned to add a jail on the site.

We both knew that the riverfront enjoyed no master plan or vision. It fell victim to the mean and expedient interests of powerbrokers. A certain kind of willy-nilly, opportunist, ugliness persists, all for a few jobs.

"How does this happen?" I asked Maria.

"I don't really know," she said. "We don't have much faith in big dreams or new ideas. They might come true in other places, not here." Then she reconsidered, checking her cynicism. "Maybe it's changing. I hope it is."

Squinting into the setting sun, we could see the northerly edge of the plateau above the Ohio River, where Logstown and Legionville once stood, now dominated by closed, dilapidated factories. If Maria and I could have occupied this vantage point on June 6, 1824, we would have seen a steamboat named *Ploughboy* chugging upriver, carrying two hundred Harmony Society members and their self-proclaimed prophet George Rapp. A fire-brand and free-thinker, Rapp had been jailed for thinking too freely about Lutheranism in Germany in the late 1700s. When authorities cut him loose, he told his flock of nearly twelve thousand that he would lead them to religious freedom in America.

Pennsylvania advertised itself as a haven for religious expression, and separatists of varying stripes came in droves— Quakers, Shakers, Mennonites, Harmonists, and others. Within ten years of arriving in Philadelphia and forging their way to the frontier, they had built a thriving industrial and agricultural community north of Pittsburgh, and called it

Harmony. By 1811, the Society sustained about eight hundred members, and this roster gives us an idea of the occupations: "100 farmers, 3 shepherds, 10 masons, 3 stonecutters, 3 brick makers, 10 carpenters, 2 sawyers, 10 smiths, 2 wagon makers, 3 turners, 2 nailers, 7 coopers (barrel makers), 3 rope makers, 10 shoemakers, 2 saddlers, 3 tanners, 7 tailors, 1 soap boiler, 1 brewer, 4 distillers, 1 gardener, 2 gristmillers, 2 oilmakers, 1 butcher, 6 joiners, 6 dyers, dressers, shearers, etc., 1 fuller, 2 hatters, 2 potters, 2 warpers, 17 weavers, 2 carders, 8 spinners, 1 rover, 1 minister of religion, 1 schoolmaster, 1 doctor, 1 storekeeper with 2 assistants, and 1 tavernkeeper with 1 assistant." (Karl J. R. Arndt, *George Rapp's Harmony Society 1785-1847*)

In 1814, they sold Harmony to the Mennonites and moved to Indiana, where they accommodated more new arrivals from Germany and built *New* Harmony on the banks of the Wabash. Again, in a single decade, they built an impressive frontier town—185 stone buildings amidst lush gardens. Still restless for a true paradise, they sold all twenty-four thousand acres of New Harmony to the Welsh utopian philosopher, Robert Owen, and bought a better-situated thirty-two hundred acres surrounding the ruins of Logstown and Legionville.

The Harmonists' counter-migration away from the frontier was one of the first harbingers of America's Industrial Revolution: a smoke-belching steamboat running against the current. Until then, everything and everyone had traveled *down*river, or, at great effort poled up the river in the shadow of its banks.

They came ashore at French Point, hauled their gear down the gangway and faced a steep embankment about seventy feet high. Pleased by the high banks and flat stretch of land above, George Rapp wrote: "All of us believe that this is one of the healthiest places in all America."

A century unlike any other had begun. Until then, the explorers and settlers, the trading nations of Logstown and the legions who trained under Mad Anthony, had left few scars behind and took very little away. Those on the *Ploughboy* had different ideas. In that river running beneath me and my kid sister, they saw milk, and on that riverbank to our right, they saw honey.

George Rapp infuriated typical capitalists. He sought only to practice Christian communal living as described in the Bible. He had no evangelical aims, sought no converts, and had plenty of members. Harmonists had begun to hold common property and a communal purse before moving to America, and extended the practice of communal ownership to Harmony and New Harmony.

Members agreed: If they chose to leave, they had no claim to property, possessions, or reimbursement. For those concessions, all of their physical needs were met and they were granted access to the religious and educational benefits of the Society.

So, they were early communists. But the term hadn't been coined yet. Their belief that Christ would return made them Adventists and more specifically "millennialists" because, like the Shakers and other sects, they were convinced that Christ would show up by 1900. Rapp insisted that Christ could appear at any moment to live with him and his people, if only they could form a community worthy of him.

One of the first facts I knew about the people who once lived in the preserved village on the north end of Ambridge was that they weren't allowed to have children. As a Catholic boy, that notion seemed odd in the extreme. Priests practiced celibacy, but they weren't married, and these Harmonists were. The belief of ideal worthiness in the eyes of a soon-to-return

Christ stems from German mystic Jakob Boehme's particular reading of the Bible, asserting Adam was a "bi-une" creature in the image and likeness of God, with no sex organs, and he fell from grace when the female aspect of him separated. Although we know Rapp had sex organs of his own, he believed that he could achieve the God-like state of the uncorrupted Adam by shelving those organs, so to speak. As a celibate, he intended to set an example for others to follow that would push the world back toward universal harmony.

Celibacy in exchange for harmony: a control freak's dream, something like repression for peace, denial for unity. Historians disagree as to whether Rapp insisted upon chastity, or, by modeling it in his own marriage and extolling the virtues of the practice for the good of the soul and the Society, the members willingly adopted it. Adopting celibacy carried theological weight with many separatists, including the Shakers, and it made short-term economic sense, too.

Ironically, the practice ran directly counter to the ideas of the most influential economic theorists of the time—Adam Smith and Thomas Malthus—who insisted the need for food and the need for sex could be satisfied through propagation. An air thick with theories swept news of the Harmonists' celibacy across the Atlantic.

Lord Byron devoted a passage in *Don Juan* (canto 15) to ridiculing Rapp. Byron's high-profile scorn shows how Rapp's fame had grown, and that he had become what one historian, Karl van Arndt, called "the greatest communist of his age." Byron directed his mockery not so much toward celibacy, but toward the idea that practicing it would achieve harmony.

While Byron poked fun at Rapp, Frederick Engels praised him in his articles and in his letters to Karl Marx. All of this attention paid to Rapp would eventually fall into the deep creases of history, but throughout the 1800s, Rapp and his community influenced America's writers and philosophers and became a powerful commercial enterprise.

Dramatically seizing the moment of his arrival in 1824, "Father" Rapp, as he was known to the men unloading the *Ploughboy* at French Point, clambered up the steep bank to the plateau above and revealed his most recent directive from the Almighty. He should name the new town "Economy" from the Greek for "household," specifically the Phillipians' "Divine Economy"—referring to the household of Father, Son, and Holy Ghost. A town with such a name would throw its doors open to the returning Christ. How could he resist this magnificent stretch of land, rimmed by gentle slopes and ridges, blessed with virgin forests and riverbed soil, perfect for vineyards and orchards?

Mulberry trees were among the first cultivations—ten thousand of which would soon line the streets. The mulberry leaves came to feed a half million silkworms, rumored to have been smuggled in from China, allowing the Harmonists to eventually dominate the American silk market.

From its beginning, Economy had a different focus than the previous two settlements. George Rapp scouted and selected Harmony and New Harmony for their agricultural advantages, allowing the Harmonists to become self-sufficient. Their manufactures could be sold only after they had clothed and equipped themselves. In Economy, acres of grain, feed, vineyards, and orchards made self-sufficiency simple, and their industrial production, everything from whiskey and wine to cotton, linen, and silk textiles, found better markets than in Indiana. The Society supplied passing frontiersmen and shipped goods to customers in twenty states and eleven foreign countries.

While Rapp tended his flock with increasingly bizarre and tyrannical philosophy, his adopted son, Frederick, ran most of the Society's business. He made the Society a force in Pittsburgh's booming business community, commissioning its own steamboat and arranged for all forms of transportation heading west to wharves and depots in Economy.

By staying downriver from Pittsburgh, the Society's manufactured goods could avoid the metropolitan bottleneck and ply the swift Ohio all the way to the Mississippi. The farmland surrounding Economy could easily feed the town and its inhabitants, as well as furnish materials—flax, silkworm cocoons, grapes, rye, timber, coal, and clay—for their industries and buildings. In just two years, Economy became a village of tidy brick houses and shady streets surrounded by pastures with large, bustling factories heated and driven by steam.

In all of their settlements, the Harmonists built a hotel, and in Economy travelers coming from Pittsburgh heard about the Harmonists' hospitality, their honesty, fine wines, exquisite silks, and excellent food. They found peace in the Harmonists' demeanor, beauty in their gardens, lanes, and orchards, culture in their music, and inspiration in their industry. Visitors took the Harmonists' products, as well as their confidence and inspiration, with them into the western lands. Even in its infancy, Economy hosted visitors that included notable social theorists, scholars, royalty, Supreme Court justices, and governors. Later, the Harmonists received and entertained two presidents.

With business agents throughout the country and an incomparable workforce, the Society began drawing criticism from competitors, who charged it with cornering markets and monopolistic practices. In those freewheeling days of speculation and empire-building, this tightly knit cloister of communists had the capitalists crying for mercy. One Pittsburgh newspaper called for the state legislature to forcibly dissolve the Society. But Frederick Rapp had played by the rules, gained prestige, and maintained a personal relationship with the powerful Henry Clay.

In 1830, a combination of Andrew Jackson's attack on the federal banking system and a land rush on the frontier, had investors abandoning manufacturing for cheap real estate, causing a surplus of imports, and threatening the solvency of the young United States. The Harmony Society would have none of this get-rich-quick scheme.

Among Frederick's political allies and friends was Nicholas Biddle, owner of the Second United States Bank in Philadelphia, which held the Society's funds. Facing a nationalization of his bank by Jackson in 1836, Biddle sold his estate and melted down all of his silver and gold, sending the Society its balance of $550,000 in hard money—by some accounts, more than the federal treasury had at the time.

This cache of custom-minted coins became extremely valuable when the real estate boom crashed and Jackson issued an order demanding gold or silver in payment for government land. Most investors had only bushels of paper currency. Banks called in their loans and a panic swept the nation; nearly half of all banks crashed, and businesses in New York City lost one hundred million dollars in two months.

Economy, though, easily rode out The Panic of 1837 and the six years of depression that followed. At one point, the Society was secure enough to loan the City of Pittsburgh money for a new water system. George Rapp saw the economic calamity as yet another omen of the Second Coming. In his dotage, it seems that every event portended the validity of his prophecies.

He waited, sermonized, and fought off lawsuits from exiting

members until, in 1847, at the age of ninety, he died. The man who in many renderings resembles a tree gnome with a long beard and pointy hat, died waiting for a day that never came. But his worldly visions exceeded all expectations.

In addition to Rapp's fame and infamy, he slept every night since 1837 atop a vault sunk into the floor of his bedroom that held Biddle's shipment of gold and silver. His spiritual certainty, esoteric studies, and infectious belief system had given rise to a life of manic building and radical behavior. Lacking a new generation to forget his transgressions and hold him aloft, the evidence of his genius was bound in cold bricks and hard currency.

Without Rapp's patriarchy hanging over them, the Harmonists could finally govern themselves. With its profits, the Society continued its tradition of supporting other religious communities—Shakers, Zoarites, and Inspirationists in the Amana colonies. And it bought land in Haifa, anticipating Zionism and the communal practices of the *kibbutz.*

By various accounts, the Harmonists brought slaves with them from Indiana who were released once in Economy. Members developed Abolitionist leanings and Abraham Lincoln became a hero among them. Too old to serve in the Civil War, and pacifistic besides, the Harmonists supplied the Union army with food, clothing, blankets, money, and whiskey.

At the time of Romelius Baker's death in 1868, the Society had operated mills throughout the Ohio and Beaver valleys and owned all the surrounding land, including what would become the city of Beaver Falls. In addition, it tapped the hillsides and ravines for coal and other mineral deposits, building short-line railroads to transport the booty. Succeeding Romelius Baker, the Society's Jacob Henrici consolidated its rail system and became president of the Pennsylvania & Lake Erie Railroad.

Visitors to Economy came via its own trains. He also extended the Harmonists' real estate holdings north, toward Lake Erie—where the Society would multiply its wealth by controlling a natural resource that came to dominate the global economy.

Long before the Civil War, most of the Society members were growing too old to work in the factories and fields. They hired more employees and sold off the silk and cotton mills, as well as the whiskey distillery. But when Edwin Drake struck oil with the world's first oil well, in Titusville in 1859, the Society owned much of the land surrounding his discovery. Drake was a scientist, not a prospector, and deserted Pennsylvania once he finished his project. The Society saw oil's potential immediately. It invested heavily in drilling, and within a year, from its headquarters in Tidioute, the Economy Oil Company pumped out more than fifty barrels a day. In the following year, it extracted seven hundred fifty thousand barrels of crude into barrels manufactured by Harmonists and carried away on Harmonist rails and trains.

With technical expertise, the Society began drilling closer to home, in the fields that had been pastures, in the streambeds that had watered their livestock. Around the turn of the century, one hundred fifty derricks bobbed for oil and gas on land around Economy. A new bonanza had begun.

Jacob Henrici led the Society to become an enviable institution to those who might be immune to envy: the Shakers and the Vanderbilts. Within such pious and capitalistic company, the Society gained additional notice as a model of prosperous communism. Yet its foundation was eroding as the century neared its end without Christ showing up, and with most of its original members dying off. By the late 1800s, employees outnumbered members by five to one. They were paid in the same way as the members—with free housing, food, a small stipend, and education—but they all submitted to the Society's harsh rules in an effort to gain membership and a stake in the fortune.

Two such employees were John and Susanna Duss. After decades of pleading and political maneuvering, the music teacher and his housekeeper wife wheedled their way into caregiving positions for the final, doddering, elders. Through documents signed on deathbeds, the couple gained control of the Society and closed the membership doors behind them. In 1893, John Duss named himself president, wrapping his hands around six million dollars (roughly equivalent of $140 million today) in assets.

Soon after, he used Society funds to produce one of his operettas in Madison Square Garden, including a watery replica of Venice, paying for it to be performed by the New York Metropolitan Opera. On the following day, a reviewer for the *New York World* wrote: "Ego was the chief characteristic of the Duss concert."

With angry members and employees filing suits against him, Duss wanted to cash out. In 1902, J. P. Morgan consolidated dozens of steel companies into United States Steel. One of its subsidiaries brought together twenty-eight bridge companies to form the American Bridge Company, which became the largest steel fabricator in the world. Duss made a deal with Morgan to locate the American Bridge Company on 130 acres of land along the river. Duss then sold an additional twenty-five hundred acres to the company's newly formed real estate speculation branch—The Liberty Land Company. American Bridge had bought itself a company town, and named it Ambridge.

Soon after selling all he could lay claim to, John Duss and his wife gathered up the fortune they held in trust and moved to Florida. The courts awarded the village of Economy to the Commonwealth of Pennsylvania for historic preservation. For a while, among immigrants who knew nothing about the Harmonists nor Duss's avarice, the self-proclaimed maestro returned for celebrations, staging musical productions and giving away nickels to children.

9

The Prurient Power of Pierogi

In a place averse to looking back, cultural traditions in Ambridge emerged through religion, song, dance, and food. Mostly food, though, because every day when it hit the table it reminded us of our origins.

Housewives in the 1960s experimented with modern food, but they fell back on what they learned from their mothers. And the kitchens in church basements and parochial schools turned out some of the best Old Country cooking. For me, the melding of food and religion came together on meatless Fridays.

Sitting at a kitchen table my father had built, I picked up my bowl to finish the sweet brown milk left behind by the Cocoa Krispies, letting myself go cross-eyed, pretending I didn't hear my mother click her tongue at my slurping. I stood up and set the bowl in the sink while checking the kitchen counter for my lunch box, and not seeing it. Oh, wow, it's Friday, I thought when it hit me—no packed lunch today.

My father sat quietly, working his daily crossword, doodling profiles of beautiful women in the margins, his usual morning meditation.

"Dad, could I have some money for *pirohi*?" Not pierogi, which is what Poles and Croatians called the handmade, stuffed dumplings, served swimming in butter and onions.

We Czechs and Slovaks had our own word.

Even though Milt would happily pay for my lunch, he insisted that I ask, as part of a larger lesson about money. "If you can't ask for it, maybe you don't need it," he would say, explaining that when he went to the credit union or the bank for a loan, he had to ask; they didn't just give it to him.

He smiled and dug into his front pocket, coming up with a fistful of change.

"How much?"

"Thirty-five cents." Enough to feed a nine year-old.

He held out a calloused hand and reminded me to take enough for milk. "Sixty-five for me," Mark said as he swaggered in. He was three years older. My father whistled low in mock-disbelief and snapped each coin on the Formica table one at a time. Betty jerked away from the counter where she had been buttering toast, annoyed by the snapping of the coins. Mark kissed her and she handed him a glass of grape juice. He downed it, grabbed the change and two slices of toast.

Watching quietly behind his empty bowl, Chris, who was just finishing first grade, looked up at Mark with wide eyes and announced, "*Pirohi* today!" Mark swallowed and said "Well, it is Friday, doofus." With that, Betty, known for her prickly morning moods, popped Mark behind the right ear. He shook it off, and after a hurried round of kisses, we headed out the back door on a typical Friday morning, going off to school with more freedom than on the other days of the week. None of the Catholic schools provided everyday lunches, but their churches raised money with *pirohi*, or *pierogi*, or *pirozhki*. On Friday, without lunchboxes or bags, I had a free hand with which to gesture and swat, pick up pebbles and throw them at street signs, on our way to the bus stop.

Streets in the neighborhood ran like creeks to a river that

was the main road. Out of the tiny households came kids with an array of European surnames: Marcia Sokil, with her fine and even Ukrainian features, would get off the bus at Sts. Peter and Paul; Dave Duplaga, a Pole, would say goodbye in front of St. Stanislaus, Bobby Cipriani at St. Veronica's.

Swaying like a drunk around the corner, the bus skidded onto the gravel shoulder. It was a heap, an eyesore even in its industrial surroundings. Tosta's Bus Company served the parochial schools, hauling their students in broken-down buses of two designs: the salvaged city bus, and the retired tour coach. The city buses, with fare boxes, shiny handrails, outdated billboards and cables for requesting a stop, were like rolling funhouses. In contrast, the coaches were dark and quiet, with overhead luggage racks and high, reclining seats that were threadbare and torn.

All the buses had rusty floorboards with holes big enough to see the road, but too small to lose a foot through, and gearboxes that just caught. The drivers, all mechanics, wore greasy jumpsuits and smelled like garlic, motor oil, and sweat. One smoked a pipe while he drove, stuffed with what could only have been plain old oak leaves.

"Oh…God…no," I groaned when the door swung open and smoke rushed out like a late commuter. I saw the goofy smile of the green immigrant, holding the door lever with the same hand that held his goosenecked pipe, its mouthpiece crushed from his few remaining molars.

Inside, a cloud hung over the luggage rack. The usual choke of moldy seats and exhaust fumes that seeped up through the floor was overwhelmed by the smoldering trash in the driver's pipe. We made gagging sounds and laughed, but the driver only watched us and smiled with his pipe in his teeth. Most days I prayed for the bus to break down. My hopes sprang from the frequency with which it happened—first a loud clunk, then a whimper from below, the driver cussing and wrestling the rig onto a lawn or a sidewalk. They never called for help, preferring to slide their toolboxes stored under their seat and fix it themselves.

On Fridays, though, my brothers and I wanted a smooth ride. By the time the bus wheeled to the curb in front of Divine Redeemer, I noticed Chris's vacant stare and gaping mouth. The poor little aromatically sensitive guy, who ran from the house to escape offensive cooking odors, had turned khaki. I yanked our bookbags from the luggage rack and escorted Chris down the aisle and stairs. On the sidewalk, he doubled over and gulped the fresher air while I stood behind him, throwing my head back and inhaling like a hound in a stiff breeze. That's when I caught it. The scent of Friday shot to my salivary glands. When two nuns pushed open the churches' oak doors, even the latent incense gave way to the embrace of butter and onions.

During Mass, the promise and seduction became unbearable. My stomach clawed toward its quarry while I knelt through the long Latin consecration. I stared at the ornamental sacristy and my eyes glossed over, seeing Jesus feeding hordes of followers by multiplying pirohi instead of loaves and fishes. Or my gaze landed on the soft white mound of Monica Halicek's top vertebra. How its contours transported me, how its roundness resembled a tender potato pirohi.

Rising for the Our Father, I examined my conscience for any transgressions that might keep me from momentarily stemming my cravings with the appetizer that was communion. The unleavened wafer seemed a poor substitute for the flesh it presumed to replace. A better choice, I thought, would have been a slice of pepperoni.

Friday mornings dragged. Through religion, geography, and history lessons, I learned only forbearance. Even the nuns admitted their cravings and their secrets for coping: muttering mantras like "Jesus, have mercy on me"—*ejaculations*, they called them (setting up real teenage confusion down the road)—until the moments of weakness passed.

Billy Evans poked me in the back while Sister Tomasina answered a knock at the door. "How many you gettin'?" he asked.

"A half dozen," I whispered out of the corner of my mouth, careful not to turn around.

"I'm gettin' a *whole* dozen." Of course you are; you're fat.

When noon arrived, Sister Tomasina opened the door and the full force of cooking odors washed over us. She cuffed her sleeves and folded her thick, hairy forearms as she stood in the doorway and watched the younger kids file toward the basement. I squirmed in my seat, fishing out the coins and slapping them on my desk for a final count. Satisfied, I cupped my hand at the edge of the desk and slid the coins into it, except for the nickel that bounced off my thumb and fell to the tile floor, found its edge and rolled all the way to the back wall, where it disappeared between a row of bookbags.

Billy noticed and we were both tracking the nickel when Sister Tomasina must have signaled the class to rise and form a queue. Caught by surprise, I spun and stood, tipping over my chair. While righting it, I turned to see the angry nun hustling toward me. Her black robes billowed like a crow descending on roadkill. She took me by the ear and dragged me, sidestepping, to face the blackboard two inches away. When I dared to look sideways, I saw Billy being flung ear-first to my side.

I closed my eyes and memorized the color of the bookbags the nickel had rolled between: red and powder blue. But I doubted I'd have a chance to retrieve it. I might end up staying at the blackboard throughout lunch. Sister Tomasina's heart had long ago been removed, we theorized, frozen and broken into particles that, when added to torpedoes, made them more deadly. Maybe she'd let us go later, when the entire school had eaten the best pirohi varieties. Billy seethed. I would pay for this on the playground.

As our classmates marched out, the sweet aroma intensified and God's own forgiving breath must have swept in and subdued the nun. She ordered us to catch up with the others, but before we escaped she drew a four-foot pointer from the folds of her apron and sliced the air behind us, cracking both of our buttocks simultaneously.

The sting made us hop. But we were giddy as we started down the stairs and Billy elbowed me hard enough to knock me into the rail. That was it; retribution delivered. He didn't hold grudges. Besides, we were dropping into the most overwhelming sensual pleasure either of us would know until puberty, with a narrow escape behind us.

The pupils, as we were called, filed into a bright multipurpose room filled with long tables, folding chairs, and noisy pirohi hogs. This feast was open to the public, and local workers on their lunch breaks sat along the west wall. Kids filled half of the tables in the vast middle, and along the east wall, facing the room, sat a brigade of silver-haired grandmothers. They carefully spooned fillings—mashed potato, sauerkraut, cottage cheese, and *lekvar*, a prune preserve—into the disks of dough they cradled in their floury hands. They folded the edges together and pinched the semicircular dumplings into shape.

The pinchers would seldom rise. Other volunteers rolled out the dough and cut it into circles with teacups, or mixed fillings and delivered them to the pinchers in heaping bowls, then returned to harvest the finished pirohi.

Pinching and chatting in Slovak or Czech to the friends who flanked her, my grandmother, Anna Rosol, found my face and smiled, flashing perfect false teeth. I broke free of my classmates, now dazed in pirohi nirvana, and scrambled behind the pinchers—"Hi, Mrs. Hovanec, Mrs. Yaniga, Mrs. Duda, Mrs. Sinchak, Mrs. Tabachka"—until I reached my grandmother's strong arms and soft cotton apron. She kissed me and hugged me hard, pressing her wrists into my back. Her hands, kept chaste for touching food, flew away from me. She was careful like that.

By now, Billy had reached the serving line and I had to hurry. I patted the coins in my pocket and sorely missed that nickel. I suppose I could have asked my grandmother for one, but I knew she was too poor. If she were to give it to me, she'd probably walk home instead of taking the bus. Still, the shortfall forced me to reconfigure my usual order, maybe cutting out the lekvar, its mellow sweetness made sophisticated when it met salt, pepper, butter, and onions. I hated quandaries such as these.

Just as I was about to pick up a plate, a hunchbacked woman in a dark print dress emerged from the kitchen lugging a giant bowl of snowy cottage cheese. She saw me at once, cried my name, and set the bowl down. She wiped her hands and grabbed my face, mashing a kiss on my lips before pushing me away and tugging at the ear still tender from my trip to the blackboard. Like a magician, she let go and presented me with a shiny quarter in the palm of her hand.

Grandma Hertneky, an osteoporotic angel, always greeted me in public with a gangway flourish—even though I saw her nearly every day. Her gypsy drama, in greeting, feeding, scolding, mourning, or scaring, never subsided.

She counterposed Grandma Rosol, whose serene demeanor shrouded her in ethereal gauze.

Now I was flush. I knew all the ladies wielding spoons, too, and one scooped four glistening potato pirohis onto my plate. Then I boldly ordered two kraut to go with my usual two lekvar, forcing me to hold the plate with both hands. Searching for a seat, I saw Chris, nose-down, all business. I also spotted Mark, who had just cruised in with the upperclassmen and stood on his tiptoes to assess my plate, as if he might cross the room and steal it. He winked at me.

With the long-awaited aroma buttering my face, I found Billy and sat, just before my knees were about to buckle from excitement. I freed my fork from its napkin wrapper, grabbed the salt and pepper, checked the caps for cruel jokes, and seasoned my little treasures. With my fork, I cut the firm potato pillow in half, exposing the fine filling placed there by ancient hands, refined through generations of argument, fulfilled by sunlight, pitchforks, and cauldrons of boiling water. I flipped its gaping side down in a pool of butter and smeared it across the plate.

The first bite made me close my eyes. The multipurpose room fell silent and every cavity in my head absorbed a humble gift composed of elements that sang secret lyrics to notes along an archetypal scale, a harmony to my subconscious. In my pirohi rapture I could be lost and found, week after week, even when I reached the age when ardent kisses tried to surpass it, and never really could.

10

Life As They Found It

In a single year, J. P. Morgan used his industrial, financial, and political clout to build the American Bridge Company and Ambridge as a "smokeless" community set apart from the filthier, steelmaking precincts of nearby Pittsburgh. He invited only manufacturers that shaped and assembled the steel. When the company put out a call for workers, they flocked in from the rural South, Europe, Canada, and Mexico. The new immigrants who passed the Harmonists' orchards and vineyards looked upon Economy, the German enclave at the northwest corner of town, with awe, inspired that they, too, could build Heaven on Earth in this land. And what was true in 1804 would be true in 1904: The new arrivals invested their own vision of Utopia in powerful men who courted their belief.

The Bridge Company's real estate arm, Liberty Land Corporation, developed a prototypical company town. After completing the American Bridge office building—a brick monstrosity where my father worked as a draftsman for thirty years—the company laid out a leafy park that ran beside the river. Along the park, American Bridge built spacious houses for its executives. One block back sat smaller houses for foremen and supervisors. Farther back were row houses for laborers.

Construction hit a feverish pitch, matching the company's instant success. Demand for bridges and buildings climbed every day, and American Bridge trained its laborers and steelworkers to fabricate segments of structures that could be loaded on rail lines and barges. The company made its own barges to transport its finished pieces.

But the rush into operation demanded that Liberty Land throw up tenements for new workers. At the southernmost edge of town, nearest the Bridge Company, these four-story structures soon overflowed with immigrants, most of them Greeks. First Street stood as the counterpoint to idyllic Economy, thirteen blocks north. The crush of humanity situated on First Street, its chaos and nascence, made it seem like a world away, yet it thrived with the same determination the Harmonists possessed when they arrived. For decades, this avenue of tenements held its distinction as the town's oldest ghetto, the place most workers wanted to leave as soon as possible. Some striking scenes of life on First Street hang in museums throughout the country, captured by noted Works Progress Administration photographer, Arthur Rothstein.

Residents of the lower-numbered streets of town could reach the mill within minutes on foot. New factories followed closely behind the Bridge company—H. K. Porter Locomotive Company, National Metal Molding Company (eventually, National Electric), and The Central Tube Company, makers of pipe for transporting oil. It was hard to imagine a more hospitable place for heavy industry—with oil and gas wells operating on the site and hopeful laborers lining up at the gates. At Economy's peak in the 1850s, roughly nine hundred residents lived there under the care of the Harmony Society. By 1900, their numbers had fallen to 620. Once the industries and speculators got going, the population of Ambridge shot to 5,205 by 1910.

More houses were built as the new immigrants poured in and staked themselves by mortgage, credit, new babies, and old-fashioned loyalty to their employers. They established toeholds, and later brought in their families, friends, and their fellow countrymen. Several families lived under one roof until each could buy a house of their own, often within sight of one another. Ethnic islands formed and churches grew in their midst.

Ten new congregations formed before 1910—Baptists, Jews, Protestants, Roman Catholics, and Greek Orthodox. Soon, Ambridge became notable for the density of its churches and bars.

By 1920 the population more than doubled, to 12,730. The gentle hills that once shimmered with barley and wheat, the smart orchards of the Harmonists, were stripped and decked with massive brick and metal factories, smokestacks and gantry cranes. Forges and sheet metal plants, more makers of pipe and rails and machinery, snapped up inexpensive land. Their loading docks and railroad sidings formed tributaries that snaked toward the river where barges and freight trains carried away megatons of metal.

Amid the fury of this building boom on the east bank of the Ohio, two steelmaking magnates joined in erecting a massive integrated steel mill on the opposite side of the river. The Jones & Laughlin Steel Works gobbled up mile after mile of shoreline, producing beams, billets, bars, cans, wire, sheets, rolled steel—nearly every imaginable finished product—upwind from Ambridge, smothering the claim of "smokeless."

The town of Aliquippa grew up around J&L, but couldn't grow fast enough. Workers were needed from the Ambridge side of the river. With a bridge-maker for a neighbor, J&L forged the steel for a bridge that would connect it to Ambridge, and shipped the beams and girders one mile up the river to American Bridge for fabrication. The two companies finished the Woodlawn Bridge in December of 1927, allowing the communities to draw on each other's labor pool by making the crossing over the Ohio River a five-minute walk.

We could see all of the American Bridge Company and Ambridge, as well as the river and most of J&L, from my grandparents' house that sat on a steep hillside. We could pick out the Bridge Company office building and hear the whistles that marked the shift changes. The noon whistle meant my father would soon arrive for lunch.

Like most European-stock workers who endured the Great Depression, my father's parents knew how to make the most of their small plot of land. They maintained an intensive vegetable patch, grew grapes, cared for an apple tree, a pear tree, and three cherry trees. All of the fruit was eaten in season or preserved. They also raised a few chickens. When they weren't tending their domestic food supply, they were out foraging— for dandelion greens, berries, wild nuts, medicinal roots, and fish. Come to think of it, they lived very much like bears.

At several points in the summer, my grandparents needed help with harvesting, and child labor was as good, and sometimes better, than adult help. Betty, stretched to her last nerve by a house full of kids all summer, often posed a leading question to my grandparents during their nightly visits. She might inquire about the ripeness of the wild elderberry crop, hoping my grandfather would say something like "They're out, ready. Just need to get 'em." With that, she'd see a chance to unload at least one of us for a night, or two, or three.

My grandfather always rose before dawn, and I emulated him by hopping out of bed as soon as I heard him stir. He'd set a percolator on the stove and I'd go out to help him gather eggs and pull weeds out of the garden, returning to a kitchen bathed in the aroma of coffee. He would sit in his usual chair and crack open a paperback while I grabbed a book and followed his example. In spite of his meager education, and perhaps because his uncle had headed west to become a rancher, my grandfather devoured Western novels, especially those by Louis L' Amour and Zane Grey.

When the trees were full of fruit, one or both of my brothers would also sleep over, and after breakfast we climbed into the trees with coffee cans strung around our necks for cherries, or old pillowcases we filled with apples. We used cans nailed to sticks to pull off hard-to-reach apples and pears, with my grandfather on the ground filling the baskets. But I preferred picking wild fruits like elderberries and blackberries in places my grandfather returned to year after year and scouted during the off months.

On days when we worked around the house, we cleaned up for lunch and sat on the porch to wait for my father to join us soon after we'd hear the chorus of noon whistles rise from the factories on the riverfront. I looked down the hill, only a few blocks below, to see our parish church and its school, once attended by both of my parents, and where my siblings and I would go, too. Our school, our spiritual and social center, our relatives and source of livelihood, could all be reached within minutes. Milt came for lunch nearly every day. But, as a statement of self-sufficiency, he brought sandwiches my mother had packed for him in the morning.

Beneath the sky-lit roofs of the bridge company, men and women cast millions of rivets, bolts, fittings, and specialized pieces of steel. Some rode crane hooks and beams that hovered into place while catching red-hot rivets tossed from furnaces on the ground, placing them into holes that matched beam to beam. Others stood beneath showers of sparks, welding heavy plates into position, plumes of acrid smoke rising around them. Ear-splitting collisions rang through the shipping bays and joined the metallic cacophony that filled the valley.

My father spent his days bent over vellum sheets filled with drawings that showed how the beams and plates fit together with precise measurements, the rivet placement and the thickness of the steel. He worked side-by-side with other draftsmen, all former soldiers and sailors like him, who had served time in the mills or bypassed them, taking their math and drawing skills into the American Bridge drafting rooms. They were organized in "squads" and sat behind tall oak tables in a vast pea-green room, illuminated by long lines of humming fluorescent lights. My father constantly worried over accuracy and the potential expense of his mistakes. Squad bosses circulated among the tables, cracking the whip, in a way, pushing the men to draw, figure, and double-check faster.

Sheet by sheet, piece by piece, they detailed the Verrazano Narrows Bridge, the Sears Tower, and the Astrodome. During its eighty-three years in Ambridge, American Bridge fabricated the skeletons of the Empire State Building, the Chrysler Building, and the Woolworth Building in Manhattan, the Hancock Towers in Chicago and Boston, the San Francisco Bay Bridge, and thousands of other bridges and structures. During World War II, they built five thousand troop-landing barges and 120 tank-transport ships. Each one splashed into the Ohio River amid fanfare and prayers that it would help win the war.

My father's family had landed in Baltimore from Hungary. They were typical of the millions whose crossings from Europe were undocumented. My great-grandparents and their children settled into a crowded triple-decker in rural

West Virginia where my grandfather entered the coal mines at age twelve. They came from a village in the Carpathian Mountains, called Hertnik. Talk about having a place define you. Maybe one of the reasons I feel such a strong connection to Ambridge, and to places in general, comes from identifying my name with a particular place.

My grandfather escaped the mines and West Virginia in the early 1900s when Ambridge exploded with industry. His parents sold their boarding house near the coal fields and his father came north to work at American Bridge. He arranged work for his oldest son.

One morning, my grandfather and I were on our way to pick blackberries. "Pap," I started, from the passenger seat of his red 1955 Biscayne, "did you ever work at the bridge company?"

He sighed and looked out the window, away from me. He couldn't wait to settle into a patch of high briars at least fifty yards away from me and my inquiries.

"Yep," he said, adding "for one day." Saying four words probably made him feel like he was flapping his gums. Still, he must have known I'd have a follow-up.

"Why? What happened?"

"Saw a girder cut a man in half," he blurted. The stunning visual shut me up.

He found safer work that would take only two of his fingers in thirty years, as a die-maker at National Electric—an essential wartime job that kept him off the battlefields of Europe. He soon found jobs at the plant for his six brothers and sisters, and the family reunited in Ambridge. His bride, whose family had come to Pittsburgh from Czechoslovakia, joined him, his parents, and his siblings in an apartment on Sixth and Melrose.

Like most new arrivals in Ambridge, my father's family quickly found their European countrymen. They joined the

Slovak-speaking congregation at Divine Redeemer and kept their Hungarian-Gypsy roots to themselves. The church frowned on their superstitions and mystical beliefs—in ghosts, monsters, or magic—but they weren't ashamed, just alone. For all the ethnic European churches in Ambridge, Hungarians were on their own, especially those with a tinge of Romany in their bloodlines. They assimilated into a congregation that spoke a language most familiar to them—Polish, Ukrainian, or, in our case, Slovak.

Ambridge had much in common with the steel towns elsewhere in western Pennsylvania. When the mills opened, they were owned by old-stock American families mostly from England and Germany, and were managed by their peers. These bare-knuckles businessmen, writes John Bodnar in *The Ethnic Experience in Pennsylvania*, recruited Hungarians because they were "cheaper and more docile material."

White English speakers—Scots and Irish—were favored by the owners and supervisors and assigned the cleanest, safest jobs. Black English speakers were consigned to the hot, gaseous coke ovens, a bona fide circle of Hell. All the other filthy and dangerous jobs were given to those who could not be understood: Italians, Greeks, Slavs—Slovaks, Czechs, Poles, Croats, Serbs. Discrimination against African Americans, Italians, and "hunkies" (considered a friendlier slur than "hun," for all Slavic people) resulted in an elaborate web of segregation and tension.

In many ways, ethnic life in Ambridge, with all of one nationality working in a single department in the mill, worshipping at the same church, supporting merchants within each neighborhood, was more Balkanized and less culturally diverse than life in the immigrants' home countries. In Hertnik, Hungarians, Slovaks, Czechs, Poles, Gypsies, and

Austrian nobility lived side by side. Conversely, in Ambridge, each nationality had its own church, school, grocery, bars, and social clubs. According to John Hoerr, who described immigrant life in *And the Wolf Finally Came*, the separation and segregation played into the hands of the mill owners, who used their authority in the mills to manipulate community leaders. The early unions failed at bringing the neighborhoods together for common benefit partly because they refused to admit unskilled workers and African Americans. Hoerr points out that "lacking democratic traditions and accustomed to authoritarian leaders, the European immigrants accepted American life as they found it. Along with the blacks, they were denied promotions and confined to low-paying jobs… Without economic advancement, there could be no social mobility."

Hoerr's analysis and the research work by John Bodnar help me understand the culture that persists in Ambridge—one of powerlessness against well-established families, businesses, and entrenched political authority. As ethnic neighbors formed alliances to fight for better treatment, the labor movement finally became more inclusive and supplied an institution that could unify the immigrants in their struggle.

Even so, unions organized and demonstrated for fifty years before mounting a serious threat to business as usual. The violence that erupted on Duss Avenue during the 1933 steelworkers' demonstration had been festering for decades. Meanwhile, the dominant class of executives and foremen filled the seats on county and municipal commissions, expanding their power into political circles. As such, they supervised ethnic leaders in the mills, who, in exchange for favors, delivered blocs of voters from their neighborhoods. It was good old-fashioned ward politics, but in this case, the mill stood at the center. Patronage became a way of life.

Regardless of our heritage, we all wanted a slice of American pie and, in Ambridge that often required mutual backscratching, accepting and returning favors. The most common career advice, repeated by my own parents, was: "It's not what you know, but who you know." I hated hearing that. From what I could see, my family had done all right and knew no powerful people and didn't seek them out. Connections, they were called. They violated my sense of fairness, my American idealism. The web of connections mimicked the system of corruption most immigrants had tried to escape, only to re-create it through patronage, allowing Ambridge to be run by small-time mobsters and favorite sons. The easiest, most lawful way for a young man to earn respect and make connections was to establish a name by playing sports, and the best sport for gaining status was football.

Women raised their status by becoming cheerleaders. After they were married, they earned renown with their cooking and baking skills. My mother, a former cheerleader, foolishly paid more attention to her studies than to watching her mother cook. But she learned quickly enough by cooking for her new family every day.

I witnessed Betty's progress. After I woke from my afternoon nap, she would take me from my playpen and set me on the counter next to the stove while she singed tiny feathers off chicken pieces, chopped vegetables, or started a stew. She would tell me what she needed from the cupboard behind me, reaching over my head and giving me a whiff before she used it—nutmeg, oregano, allspice. Before long she would ask me for an herb or spice and I'd spin around to search for the right one, sniffing to make sure. She let me guess which one she wanted, based upon what smells were rising from the pan or pot—garlic, onions, carrots.

As we grew older she seldom called us into the kitchen, but if we were around, she'd give us green beans to trim or cabbage leaves to separate, cookie dough to form, batter to stir, beaters to lick. We dredged zucchini in breadcrumbs, squished raw eggs into ground beef, coming away with tiny chunks of fat up to our elbows. By the time we grew to a family of six, Betty welcomed our help, because fifteen minutes after my father walked in the door he liked to sit down to dinner.

He came home at exactly the same time every day. Willingly. Happily. Most steelworkers worked shifts, and many stopped for at least one beer on the way home, but Milt and six other guys in the neighborhood carpooled and headed straight home to their families.

On days when I stayed in town after school or went to the library, I hitched a ride home with my father and the guys. Knowing I couldn't be late, I got to his office early and bided my time in the storage alcove just inside the exit, under a bare light bulb with a cage around it. I sat on boxes of punch-cards, millions of them, about the size of number 10 envelopes with one corner clipped off and filled with tiny numbers, some of which had been punched out with rectangular holes. Their abundance and tinge of technology made me want to play with them, stacking, shuffling, drawing a series of stick figures on the backs and flipping them into jerky animation.

After a day at their drafting tables under maddening lights, manipulating squares and colored pencils, thumbing books of logarithmic tables, the men eyed the clock and rushed out when the bell rang at five o' clock. Hearing them stampede down the stairwells, I stood out of the way, atop a couple of boxes, scanning for Milt's face that I could easily spot bobbing above most of the heads. He'd see me and smile, then snatch me up, and we'd hustle out to join the others. They were talkative and happy to be on their way home to see their wives and kids; Louie had two, as did Tony and Johnny; Mike had three; Milt had four and counting.

He entered the house at 5:15 p.m. Some days he came home whistling and cheerful, other days he was merely tolerant and pleasant. If this sounds like a sunny recollection, I would betray the facts if I painted his mood as anything darker, angrier, or more prickly, especially within that first fifteen minutes. Years later, he told me that a crack in the sidewalk, three feet from the back door, spoke to him—a reminder—regardless of the pressure the day had brought, to open the door with a smile. Broken, flawed pavement might have irritated a structural draftsman to the point of repairing it, which he was entirely capable of doing. Instead, he used a random shift in the earth to reinforce a more durable structure—his gratitude for whatever might greet him in the next two seconds.

Betty's relief at that moment was palpable. Some days she could hardly hold back the tears, and she didn't. Her sounding board, her auxiliary tank of patience and sensibility, once again occupied the same room, and she mostly held her tongue until Milt had a chance to greet his kids—four of us, and then five— and settle in the kitchen with a glass of homemade wine.

These evenings followed each other like waves on a beach, and from the moment I gained any perspective on them— probably during my first summer living away from home— they supplied my earliest sense of empathy for all the kids and mothers who were treated with indifference and cruelty. I knew them. My friends and I tiptoed past their drunk, snoring fathers, as if afraid of waking a sleeping dragon. Because I can still draw into my chest the daily anticipation and joy at my own father's arrival, planted there by reliability, repetition, and rhythm, I can at least imagine life without it, life with an equally predictable sense of terror.

I could count on seeing Milt's smiling brown eyes and getting a kiss when he opened the door. As a little boy, I watched the clock in my bedroom. I often set a stockpot lid in a curve on my headboard, just below the window, to serve as the wheel of my ship. I stood on my pillow while steering the USS *John Paul Jones*, and scanned the street out front while barking orders over my right shoulder to my deckhands, or clenching a toy pipe in my teeth and singing a chantey I had picked up on television.

Captain Jim, the character who introduced television cartoons, set the tone for my adventures. He and Popeye were sailors, and Milt had been a navy man, too. I kept his sailor's manual by my bed, examining the knots, semaphore flags, uniforms, and badges. The maps enchanted me, inviting me to study every detail, the intricacies of coastlines and magnificent seas. When I surveyed the scene out my window, I saw the hills in the neighborhood as waves. I loved taking the helm when the windows steamed up on foggy afternoons and when storms swept through. A secure harbor behind me, I could face danger with confidence, sailing into the unknown. Those were glorious days on the bounding main.

Every other Tuesday we knew to finish our homework immediately after school so we could pile into the station wagon after my father came home. Payday meant dinner at McDonald's and grocery shopping afterwards. Parked under the yellow glow of the arches and the sign with the jaunty, hamburger-headed character who toted a placard with the price of hamburgers—fifteen cents—and a scoreboard showing an amazing 1,000,000 sold, Milt took our requests.

He kept the entire order in his head, something like eight

hamburgers, six cheeseburgers, seven fries, three chocolate shakes, three vanilla, one strawberry. When he left to get the food, we all jockeyed for seats in the wagon where we could eat in peace and protect our French fries. My spot allowed me to stretch out, lean against the back of the rear seat, and arrange a place-setting on top of the wheel housing.

Once Milt returned with the sacks of food and passed the packages to the appropriate recipients, we ate in silence, occasionally commenting on the other cars and noticing other families we knew. McDonald's sat along the Ohio River Boulevard, and so the river itself gave us a show. Barges bulled upriver, heaped with coal or coke or iron ore to feed J&L, the behemoth that dominated the opposite shore. Its spine, the black metal roof that ran at varying heights for six miles, was spiked with smokestacks and flues spouting blue and yellow flames. Deadly gases and particles rose in towering orange, black, and white plumes as dense as cauliflower.

More than ten thousand men and women punched into J&L every day. Among them, our neighbors and relatives smelted ores into ingots they rolled into sheets, squeezed into bars, spun into wire and wrapped into cans inside a dark universe of grime and stink and foul language. Rusty, windowless buildings hid most of the work from our view, but we kept our eyes on the furnace that shot sparks and smoke like a volcano into the twilight. At intervals, a train snaked out of a black portal, carrying slag buckets along an embankment high above the river. One after another, the buckets that looked like dumpsters as big as boxcars tipped their molten waste down the bank, each one touching off a fiery glow that rose to the cloud ceiling and ignited a shimmering path across the river toward our Biscayne wagon.

The face of glee, for me, earns its definition from the faces of my family, their heads and shoulders lit from behind by McDonald's fluorescence, and reflected in their eyes, golden streaks of prosperity, power, and hope.

Today, it's hard to imagine a slag-streaked riverbank casting a spell on a family crowded into a station wagon. Without the distraction of electronic devices, our surroundings could more easily arrest us and make an impression on us. If all we have in old age are memories, what startling instances will social media provide?

The mills were a mysterious world, at least partly because steelworkers standing around backyard barbecues never described the place—they all knew it, and their stories amounted to little more than daily accounts, anecdotes that expressed frustration, futility, or a decent practical joke. But they didn't offer details of their work. Maybe the code among returning veterans, many of whom suffered from undiagnosed PTSD, suggested they emulate strong, silent cultural icons. They had lived through a depression and a horrible war. Now, they were home, hopeful, thrilled with a sack of burgers, a frosty milkshake, a regular paycheck, and Friday night football.

11

Rough and Ready, Tough and Tender

University of Pittsburgh professor, Robert Ruck, said "Pittsburgh, more than any other city in the twentieth century, has used sports to tell its story to the world." After shouldering the industrial demands and personal sacrifices of one, if not two world wars, recent immigrants saw themselves as full-fledged Americans. And those who packed into every square inch of Ambridge began calling themselves "Bridgers."

My fellow baby boomers filled the air with footballs over the playground during recess at Divine Redeemer, and athletes took on mythic status. Our fathers set an example for hard work and a willingness to fight. All the girls applauded those traits. For every football star, hundreds of competitive boys trained to work and fight together to win.

Sports helped Bridgers transcend their ethnic rivalries and class jealousies. Churches sponsored leagues, as did mills, merchants, and social clubs. New rivalries pitted one town against another, most viciously in football. Although Ambridge High School had fielded a team since 1906, it became a dominant force with the arrival of a diminutive coach in 1928.

Growing up in Ambridge would have been vastly different without the influence of Maurice "Moe" Rubenstein. I knew his name before I could read. Born in a tough Pittsburgh neighborhood, he had nearly dropped out of Fifth Avenue

High School when a coach there recognized his speed, skill, and determination on the basketball courts and sandlots. Sports helped Rubenstein focus on his studies and stay in school, ultimately earning him a scholarship to Geneva College, a teachers' college in Beaver Falls. He came to Ambridge for his first teaching and coaching job, brimming with gratitude for the coaches that had molded his life. He vowed to do the same for the scrappy kids in Ambridge.

Rubenstein walked all over town, watching kids play ball. He learned their names and found out where they lived, and then approached their parents. George Corey, now a lawyer in California, remembers walking home from a pickup football game when a friend came to him with the news that Moe Rubenstein was at his house, talking with his mother. The coach had already established himself by that time, and Corey tore for home. "I went batshit. I couldn't believe Moe Rubenstein came to my house."

Corey weighed ninety-five pounds. Those who knew Rubenstein say that the coach found smaller players easier to coach: more motivation, energy, speed, and their confidence grew quickly every time they outplayed a bigger guy. "We were fast and we believed we could beat anybody," Corey says. "Size didn't matter. And the smaller players believed it more than the bigger ones."

Though Rubenstein stood only five feet seven inches he commanded respect by listening and speaking with careful authority. "Every word he said, we listened to," Corey recalled. "He said 'no girlfriends,' and we obeyed. He forbade us from walking home down Merchant Street where there might be gamblers and temptation, and we obeyed, finding another way home." Composed on the sidelines and nattily attired, Rubenstein handled his players with subtle manipulation. "He never yelled. *Never.*" Corey says. "If I blew a play or missed a block, he'd just look at me and hold his head, saying, 'Why do you do this to me, Georgie, why?'"

In Rubenstein's first season, his team won six games and lost only two. In his second season, the team went undefeated through eleven games, scoring 180 points and allowing *zero*. The streak continued into the following season as his team won twenty consecutive games without giving up a single point. In his first six years, his fast, gritty teams would win two championships, scoring a total of 890 points to the opponents' 113. The Bridgers dominated western Pennsylvania football— the most competitive and fertile football breeding ground in the nation.

The legend grew as the years rolled on. Hobbled by the Depression that began in Rubenstein's second year, the fans felt the sting of mass layoffs and deepening poverty, but his teams gave them something to cheer about every week. When players' parents despaired that their boys would never find work after high school, Rubenstein set his sights higher for his players. "The greatest pleasure I got in coaching," he told a reporter in 1997, "is that I could sit down and write a letter to recommend a kid to college."

And he did. Dozens of players went to some of the best schools in the nation. George Corey went to Michigan, and Len Szafaryn, the man who would become Corey's brother-in-law, went to the University of North Carolina. According to Corey, Szafaryn (pronounced *zafrin*) played in the band as a freshman in high school, and Rubenstein noticed that the kid moved gracefully and stood taller than the rest. He located the Szafaryn family house and found Len's parents sitting on the porch. Rubenstein introduced himself and asked if they would consider letting their son play football. Szafaryn's parents spoke and understood only Polish, but they knew the word "football," and they didn't like it. Not for their son. It was too rough. Rubenstein accepted their decision, but asked if he could try to talk to them again in a few months. Fine. That's fine.

After three months of tutoring from a friend, Rubenstein returned, and this time, he spoke only Polish. Len Szafaryn went on to become an All-American and was drafted by the Washington Redskins. He started for the Green Bay Packers and Philadelphia Eagles. He was one of many young men Rubenstein sent to stardom. Another, quarterback John Michelosen, led the Pitt Panthers to two national championships and became the youngest coach in the National Football League when he took over the Pittsburgh Steelers.

In his later years at Ambridge, Rubenstein became the dean of coaches in western Pennsylvania. Paul "Bear" Bryant, the legendary Alabama coach, kept in touch and made regular visits to consult with Moe. Paul Brown, the coach of the Ohio State Buckeyes and the Cleveland Browns, conferred with Rubenstein every week during the season, devising plays that the Bridgers would try on Friday nights. Rubenstein then reported the results and suggested refinements for Brown to try the following day.

Rubenstein planted football squarely in the psyche of every kid growing up in Ambridge, and the high school stadium bears his name. From my earliest days I can remember my parents bundling us up in more layers as the season went on, to cheer for the Bridgers at the stadium on Friday nights. Two bands would play; the stands would be full, and when the Bridgers in garnet and gray took the field, we threw confetti that we had made ourselves out of shredded newspapers. We saw everyone we knew. On the track that surrounded the field, politicians shook hands, and the small-time *Mafiosi* strutted in front of the grandstands, wearing topcoats over their shoulders like capes and smoking fat cigars. The public address announcer identified every player who carried the ball or made a tackle, and those names became household names. Local boys line the Football Hall of Fame—Unitas, Blanda, Namath, Ditka, Montana, Marino, Lott, and Tony Dorsett. Every young boy I knew wanted to become one of those football heroes, and we chased our dreams through backyards and empty lots.

Thus did my heroic fantasies go beyond saving the timid churchgoers from imaginary vandals or saving their souls with inspiration from the pulpit. I wanted to become a sports hero, too. I studied athletes as closely as I had studied priests and nuns. As early as first grade, I knew that piety and cleverness could work for me, and sports could make me an icon.

Another young man with an immigrant's name fueled the fantasies of my generation and breathed new life into the smoky towns surrounding us. On Tuesday, October 13, 1960, while Betty worked at the stove, I sat on the kitchen floor, peeling potatoes with a sheet of newspaper between my legs, listening to the radio. The slight lisp of the Pittsburgh Pirates' broadcaster Bob Prince articulated every curve ball and pop-up of the seventh game of the World Series against the mighty Yankees. With the score tied at nine in the bottom of the ninth, number nine, Bill Mazeroski, lifted a home run over the head of Yogi Berra. Betty slapped her spatula on the counter and covered her gasp with her hands, spun and hoisted me in the air, peppering me with kisses. Neighbors had already begun banging pots in their front yards and we grabbed spoons and saucepans and went out to join them.

A Polish, pierogi-eating hero from the coal fields of West Virginia, whose footsteps I could easily imagine following, knocked his name into the national consciousness. Mazeroski made Mickey Mantle cry. "Maz," and his recently immigrated teammate, Roberto Clemente, made me want to play baseball and work my way onto Forbes Field.

At Divine Redeemer we drew a baseball diamond with chalk on the glass-strewn playground surrounding the condemned First Ward School. Without bats or gloves, we mashed a wad of aluminum foil wrapped in masking tape to make a ball soft enough to hit with our hands and big enough to stay within the fences. The competitive games sent us back to class covered with sweat.

We played football and baseball every day after school and all day during the summer. We hit black-taped baseballs with broken bats that we mended with nails and screws. I could run to the Little League field, the site of our pickup games, within minutes, but when it came to suiting up for a real team and playing before crowds under adult supervision, I froze. With my pals I excelled, ran fast, made sliding catches, stole bases, threw strikes, and placed singles all over the field. But to put on a clean uniform, and have all these people watch farm boys throw wild fastballs at me? Uh-uh. I became the kid who waits for a walk, runs after fly balls then ducks and covers.

During my last year in Catholic school, the Bridgers won the state basketball championship, inspiring Mr. Bucik, the father of one of my Divine Redeemer classmates, to form a team. Many varsity players got their start on Catholic youth group teams, and the multipurpose room, where the *pirohi* were served, conveniently had the markings for a basketball court laid into its tiles. As clever as we were, though, at using boulders as basepads and aluminum foil for balls, basketball requires baskets. But you couldn't tell that to Mr. Bucik.

He convinced us that we could learn plenty about basketball

by practicing without baskets, and we wanted to play so badly that we went along. We ran passing and dribbling drills, then simple plays, all of which concluded in one of us heaving the ball at a square made of masking tape on the wall. Mr. Bucik urged us to practice shooting on our own, wherever we could find a hoop. We were ten kids and one adult in absolute denial of our absurdity, until our first game—a drubbing our coach blamed on lack of hustle and poor passing. We drilled harder, hoping, I suppose, to eventually meet another team that practiced without baskets.

My parents went along with Mr. Bucik's lamebrained program, but they cared little about athletics and more about character. When it came to sports, they left us alone. Though they could have strolled to the ballfield, they had chores to do and showed no interest in sitting in the bleachers with parents whose pride annoyed them. After games, when they saw that I was wearing a uniform and a lump on my forehead, they asked me how it went, and expected me to handle defeat and injury with grace and modesty.

Perhaps Betty and Milt knew more about what makes a hero than I did. "It doesn't matter if you hit home runs or strike out; you should only play if it's fun. That's why it's called 'playing,'" my mother said. She felt we had enough pressure to perform well in school, help out around the house, attend Mass, sing in the choir, serve as altar boys, and stay in "scouting." Yes, they insisted that we join the Cub Scouts and move on to Boy Scouts, attend weekly meetings, pay our dues, and head off for camping weekends. "It's good for you," my parents said, and by that they meant it taught skills built on ideals and a code—respect for nature, community, and leaders—without grueling practice sessions and long schedules of games.

Unlike the baseball getup, which commanded me to

perform in front of grownups, my scout uniform made me feel independent from adults and capable among my peers. It rewarded me for spending days in the woods, starting fires without matches, fixing machines and radios, cooking, sewing, patching a wound, a tire, or a pair of jeans, skinning a rabbit, plucking a chicken, or frosting a cake. I learned to watch, ask questions, guess, and keep trying—all while climbing trees, cutting wood, playing with fire and carrying a knife.

I didn't give a rat's ass about rank and merit badges, which indicated my destiny as more of a service model than a performance model. I liked how scouting reinforced lessons I had learned in Catholic school, but in a sectarian way. Helping an old lady across the street is concrete; the Good Samaritan is abstract. The Scout Pledge seemed more useful than the Ten Commandments. And my fellow scouts sharpened my interest in public school. In seven years my angelic classmates and I had worn out thirteen teaching nuns. I had fantasized and fidgeted through roughly 1,260 masses, had gone from tripping over the smallest altar boy cassocks to wearing the longest ones, grown bored with lighting candles, drinking sacramental wine, marching in processions, and swinging incense around caskets for tips. During communion, I became careless with the gold paten, distracted by the way the girls tilted their heads back and stuck out their pink, moist tongues. On the playground, their plaid jumpers and knee socks suddenly sent me directly into the porn section of purgatory. I knew my classmates too well and I wanted to swim in a larger pool.

Finally, at Baden-Economy Junior High, I could practice basketball in a gym with baskets. And, I could ride a yellow school bus instead of a scrapped Greyhound; I could have teachers who wore street clothes, some of whom were men, and I could eat in a real cafeteria with American food. Exiting that school bus and entering a crowded school that had no attached church, hallways with no crucifixes, and classrooms specifically devoid of ejaculations, made me feel like I'd arrived at a teen version of Ellis Island.

On the first day, I found the number of girls dizzying. I had been watching the same thirteen girls grow up for seven years, seeing them intensify from squeaky sprigs to sturdy opposites who I knew like my sisters in school uniforms. Girls at junior high wore miniskirts, peasant blouses, and culottes. They passed notes and between classes walked glued to the ribs of older boys. I found the whole scene disorienting. Sports instantly slipped on my personal hierarchy of fascination.

And yet, most of the boys draped with girls were athletes. With the dream planted firmly in mind by the Rubenstein legend and a new understanding of the perks that came with stardom, I marched right into football tryouts. I had never played the game with pads and it took me forever to dress in the locker room. My bony head swam in the helmet, obliterating most of my peripheral vision, which became a dangerous deficit when passes, tacklers, and blockers began appearing out of nowhere. Within a week, one of the guys told me that a popular girl "liked" me. Wow, I thought, the magic of football as a guarantee of success is real! Just as all the other players knew how to read playbooks and carry out assignments, they also knew that rumors about girls were to be treated with caution. They certainly knew better than to walk straight up to this girl, whom I met once, to ask if the rumor was true. Which, in my innocence, I did.

She dropped her jaw and then pressed her lips together as she fought to hold back laughter, but only for a moment. She cocked her head in a kind and sympathetic way and told me that it was just a rumor, "People do that here. Don't be offended.

It's cute that you told me." We started a friendship. The boy she wanted was already a star halfback. And they would soon become a couple.

The other boys at football practice were the sons and nephews of the local legends, and we would be meeting rivals that had made the steel valleys famous for this sport; it was like trying to make the ski team in Telluride. For weeks, I knew nothing but pain and dread throughout my days as a newcomer, but it only redoubled my determination to play organized football.

When we gathered for an introduction to the offensive and defensive playbooks, I watched guys who couldn't even pronounce "algebra" nodding their heads in recognition of diagrams that looked like Sanskrit to me. At the end of the meeting, I had no sense of what I should do on the field.

How could I—an A-student who could draw a map of Moldavia from memory and diagram Victorian sentences— be too stupid to play football? Apparently I was. Just like in baseball, the pickup games had little to do with the sport played while wearing uniforms. My confusion led to racking blindside hits as I found myself in terrible places at terrible times—points of convergence for brutes looking to bowl me over. Several other fourteen-year-olds who, like me, weighed less than the cheerleaders, suffered the same fate. Somehow, I managed to survive to make the jayvee team and play exactly two games, one against Hopewell Junior High and their star running back Tony Dorsett. Although hitting anyone running toward me at full speed frightened me, I saw him coming and wanted a piece of him, but when I finally found an angle of attack, he shook me off like a bead of sweat and trampled me. Repeatedly.

For my own safety, the coaches sat me on the bench.

Keeping up with my studies was easy compared to the demands of the nuns. I liked that I no longer sat in one classroom, in front of one teacher, all day long. But now, with every bell, an intense social mayhem reignited, and girls provided most of the sparks. Even though every conversation with my buddies ran toward sports, I privately began to think that games mattered less than girls. I wanted to meet them, talk with them, make them laugh, walk them from class to class and escort them home from the bus stop. I liked eating lunch with them, unfolding notes from them, and, within a couple of months, holding hands with one of them.

Most of the girls were obsessed with claiming, arranging exclusivity, and showing other girls that they had found a partner, an instinct that alarmed me. I resisted it, wanting no part of devotion when so much adventure lay ahead.

I couldn't wait for the first Friday night dance. Once there, I plastered myself against a wall with other boys who stood as if facing a firing squad. After watching a while, though, I saw that I could play this game. In the middle of the school's lobby a mirror-ball spun from the ceiling, adding to the psychedelic effect of massive speakers booming out Iron Butterfly and Beatles songs. A band of students set up their drums and amplifiers to play sets, but the deejay, an ultra-cool upperclassman, controlled the atmosphere. Girls giggled in clusters, shooting looks toward the boys against the walls and breaking into dances with each other. During the wildest rock numbers the boys hesitated but then drifted onto the dance floor, and I followed along, trying to mimic those around me and what I had seen on television—the go-go girls and Dick Clark's dance parties.

Dancing to rock and roll required no dance steps, just letting go, an impossible level of unselfconsciousness for nervous, sober teenagers. Most of us looked like idiots, only redeemed by a general sense of forgiveness. The counter-culture's turn away from formality left many wondering what to do. I favored Motown and profited from the rare gym class when the teachers opened the curtain between the girls' and boys' side, lined us up and dropped a needle on Temptations and Smokey Robinson records, showing us how to Cha-Cha and line dance like the Miracles and Supremes.

When the lights dimmed and a set of slow songs began, a sigh of fading inhibition fell over the room and couples wrapped their arms around each other, holding on for the sensation of each other's contours, shuffling and swaying in a sort of slow motion dirty dancing.

We had dances every Friday night, and by the third one, I had found dance partners and enough confidence to make the transition from fast to slow dances instead of running away. Once I allowed myself to fall into the clutches of Sandy Csidowicz, our lips had a way of brushing, pressing, and permitting. Too shy to make out in front of everyone, she showed me to the darker corners and alcoves off the lobby where I discovered, among other things, masses of kids who had gone missing from the dance floor and now crammed themselves into these spaces, against the walls or sitting side-by-side on cafeteria chairs, mostly just kissing and kissing and kissing, for hours.

I happily went along with the endless exchange of saliva and chafing, taking breathers to say things that couldn't be said elsewhere. Unspoken rules governed the *kabuki* that took place in those corners, and the girls who had no rules scared me. But I learned the pleasures of a new kind of play, a way to silently learn more about girls, and all kinds of ways to evoke responses, lose myself, and engage in an endless chain of wordless interest, surprise, and an addictive source of confidence. It is said that we learn through doing, and, to this day, in conversations and relationships, I still call upon that mutual swapping of attention I first encountered in those dark, edifying corners.

12

Moms Who Put Out

You would talk to Jesus Christ on the cross," Mimi Lacarno said to me as we walked away from a beach full of strangers. She hadn't meant it as praise, but as a gentle accusation. I took her point, laughed, and wrapped my free arm around her.

"You wouldn't?" I asked.

She shrugged.

"No, you wouldn't, would you? I mean, even if he walked across the lake and handed you a fish sandwich?"

"I guess I would say 'Thank you.'"

Mimi was quiet, but talked easily on the day we met at the start of a twenty-mile Walk for Hunger. Our conversation continued all the way along the Ohio River to Beaver Falls. I suppose I drew her out, but she also took me on and the day-long walk under November skies and snow squalls made me feel like we were waltzing through scenes from *Dr. Zhivago*. By the time we shed our parkas and huddled over hot cocoa, we were smitten.

Her shyness gave way to intrigue—like throwing matches at my flammable curiosity. Quiet people do that to me. A walk, or a drive, or working on a project together, requires little eye contact; thoughts have room to run and it's easier to talk.

One problem: She was my friend Vinny's sister and only fourteen years old to my sixteen, but seeing her as a kid sister allowed me to relax more with her. Still, I fought the urge to take her by the hand. For more than a year I watched her beauty and sweetness deepen, until I couldn't resist and we began a relationship I would never completely understand.

The combination of her delicate features, deep mahogany eyes, sleek onyx hair, a satin smile, and stubborn reticence drew me into a mystery that her careful lips couldn't reveal. I sort of groped around in the dark for her, trying to figure out what was on her mind, because she wasn't saying. But she always said yes when I asked her out to a movie or a meal, for a ride or a hike, quietly indulging my curiosity about everything but her.

She even went horseback riding with me, an activity that seldom pleased my dates as much as it did me. I wanted to learn about horses and found a farm where they could be rented and ridden along a circuit of trails through the woods. What could be more fun? I didn't drag anyone there; they came along willingly. When Mimi and I started up the long, rutted driveway to the barn, we were greeted by one of the stable hands—a shirtless twelve year old with a scar that ran from his throat to below his navel, as if he had been flayed. I gulped, worried that any reasonable person might take that as a warning sign. Mimi remained stoic. Her quiet calm soothed her horse, but riding also demands assertiveness, and that didn't come easily to her. Girls tend to like riding, I reasoned, but none of them asked to return to the scary farm with the barn-sour horses.

Mimi made no demands on me, which I liked because I didn't want to date her exclusively. Allowing me to take the lead, she never asked when she might see me again, or tried to arrange a regular evening or weekend day for our dates. She had seen me around school, often in the company of girls, sometimes just one, but mostly a gaggle, talking and joking as if I were one of them. If she thought I was interested in having other girlfriends, she thought I was interested in having lots of other girlfriends. And she was right. Girls were too varied and exciting for me to spend all my time with one. She knew this, and yet she was loyal to me, always ready to go out or entertain me at home, and I never saw her with another boy nor heard from her about another. She had lots of girlfriends to hang out with.

The very idea of calling a girl and asking her to go to a dance, to the zoo or the lake, to a football game or a concert, felt like an adventure. After paying for my car insurance, I spent most of my money on dating. I had great pals but seldom wasted a weekend night with them. Without looking for love or sex, my fascination with girls took over and I happily did anything they wanted to do, or not do.

When I met a girl I liked, I wanted nothing more than to hold her hand—a nervous impulse but a simple one. Hands told me what words could never tell, from the way they matched the rest of her body to the way she cared for them, and how they moved when she talked, how they gripped a cup or a fork or a stack of books. It went back to my fixation on my grandmothers' hands while they cooked and crocheted, and my father's way of working a pencil or plucking a pheasant. I kept track of a date's hands as I drove. Did they carve her words, fly all over, rest easily, were they clasped between her knees or searching along upholstery creases for comfort?

Early on, I didn't date many girls who wanted much beyond kissing, who encouraged more touching. Those were girls who put out—a term I always found funny because, even though the girls I dated didn't put out, their mothers did, in a way.

"Here," they would say the moment I walked in, "let me

put something out." When I heard that expression, it made me think of one mother who actually did put out in a carnal way for Mimi's brother, Vinny. I knew the woman (and dated both of her daughters) and she never put out so much as a single potato chip for me, but Vinny had no interest in potato chips, nor the daughters.

Food played a starring role in our lives; all ethnicities had their specialties and everyday meals, and some I could identify the moment I crossed a threshold. Mimi's mother, for instance, was an insomniac, and she put out day and night, yanking a baked ziti out of the oven at 11:30 p.m. when Mimi and I were trying to sneak in from a date. The Polish Mrs. Lacarno learned to cook Italian for the mister, forming a culinary marriage made in heaven. Sometimes she put out sausage and peppers or stuffed cabbage. She never left the kitchen, canning tomatoes or beans, sweating through August afternoons, or perched on a stool at night, smoking Larks and listening to talk radio, ready with an apple or ricotta pie.

Every Christmas Eve Mrs. Lacarno really put out. She served a feast for at least twenty guests, then mounded the table with fried smelts and *baccala*, lupini beans, nuts, cheese, nougat candies, kumquats, oranges, cookies, apples, and hemmed it all in with carafes of homemade wine. We sang and ate and flirted, and Mrs. Lacarno blushed with overwhelming joy and pride and exhaustion. When it came time for everyone to leave for midnight Mass, I'm sure she leaned back and lit a post-climactic cigarette.

Throughout high school, my pals and I often piled into one of our father's cars and visited girls we knew. We showed up without warning, but the moms usually threw their arms around us, regardless of their daughters' ennui. Three of us might show up, sit around the kitchen table and do our best to entertain the daughter and maybe one of her friends, but we saved our real charm for the moms, especially when we could smell *braciole* or stuffed artichokes, left over from dinner. All these moms had leftovers. Even if their own families were small, they grew up learning to cook for big families.

My own mother put out. By instinct, Betty pivoted after greeting a guest and flung open the fridge or the oven and soon presented God knows what: pierogies, pork chops, chocolate cake. Dishes clattered as coats were removed, and before a guest could catch his breath, he was handed a fork. The urge to feed sprang from the bottom of her maternal heart.

Then there were fathers who put out. "Try this," they insisted: salty, spicy, manly dried sausages in which "you won't find no fat," or a plateful of sautéed banana peppers they had grown themselves, smoked fish they had caught, venison they had bagged, wrapped in neat white paper, wine made in the basement, an endless parade of delicacies, served with pride.

Intense pride separated the dads from the moms. The men served trophies, masterpieces of fussy gardening or butchering, savory expressions of sweetness and heat and patience. If I asked for more, they loved me. But if I didn't, they didn't care. Their craft was for show as much as sharing.

Although the moms were proud, too, the cooking was second nature to them, and they derived most of their satisfaction from the way we dove in, the passion with which we lapped up sauces and picked up every last crumb. Then they insisted on more, sometimes refilling a plate without asking. "But, Mrs. Silverman, I already ate half the brisket!" She had another one in the oven.

The grandmothers were worse. Before I could take Angela Andolini for a Sunday afternoon drive, she stipulated that we stop to see her *nonna*, always "just for a few minutes." Greens—

collard greens, broccoli rabe, chard—whatever Vic Amoroso had fresh at his market she steeped in broth and salt pork with moony white beans. The minute I walked in, she put it out. Bowls big enough to feed a St. Bernard. After three helpings, I pleaded with Angela to say goodbye. Then the old woman would frown and shove us both out the door, yelling, "No wonder you're so skinny!"

My mom pulled the same stunt, never satisfied with my satisfaction. I could eat six or eight meatballs, but then she held the bowl in front of me again, urging me to what? Go for an even dozen? I'd groan and wave her off. She'd shrug and say, "You don't much care for my meatballs, do you?"

I heard a hint of jealousy and suspicion in her voice. She was thinking: What does Dorothy Sacco put in those meatballs he likes so much? But she was a good sport, even after she found out that Mrs. Colorito always, without fail, made me a cake for my birthday because I once told her she made the best cake I had ever tasted. I wasn't lying. It remains the best. The woman had five kids of her own, but she couldn't help herself. Standing back, away from the table, her hands folded over the front of her apron, she watched me eat and hoped her daughter was taking note.

She shouldn't have worried, not about me, anyway. I took my first restaurant job at fifteen and was cooking full meals for paying customers by seventeen. Betty had taught me how to work my way around the kitchen, and though I happily waited while women cooked for me, I more often cooked for them, or with them. My way of easing the anxiety of having someone drop in for a visit is to get them a drink and start hauling provisions out of the refrigerator. Our first ten minutes are spent in the kitchen, where we talk while I fix a platter, cover a pan and stick it in the oven, or set a pot over a flame. At home, I habitually make extra because my jobs as a line cook and sous chef have taught me the joys of turning the surplus from yesterday into an even better dish today. I need to feed, dismissing guests' protestations, not out of generosity, but out of cultural inculcation.

Life among immigrants reinforces the tendency to open doors for everyone and shove food in their faces. If I had wanted to avoid that ritual, I knew to refrain from knocking and drop a package on the doorstep, slip it into the mailbox, or take care of business by phone. Sometimes, though, another custom made a surreptitious drop-off impossible. If a friend or her mother sent me home with a dish full of gnocchi, I couldn't return it empty; it had to contain a couple pieces of pie, say, or a pork chop, which can't be left in a mailbox. So, I sheepishly knocked, hoping a child would answer, but even if it were the daughter, or the son, or the father, and they were on the phone, they'd keep talking while grabbing me by the sleeve, pulling me into the living room, and pushing me into a chair until they could end the call. Before they returned to say hello, I would hear clattering in the kitchen as they prepared to put something out.

13

A Flame That Water Fed

One Sunday before Mass, I followed my uncle Charlie into the crowded vestibule. As I waited to dip my fingers into the holy water, I noticed him cup his hands and splash the water onto his forehead.

So that's how he does it, I thought. *That's how he makes it look like he's crying.* It was a deliberate show of devotion, a bit of theater to accompany his loud singing and praying.

His parents had carried the infant Charles Blaise Cassidy across the Atlantic from Tralee on Ireland's west coast to Pittsburgh, where he stayed. He never spoke about his family in Ireland. He related what his parents had told him about the crossing, and remembered only diesel fumes and the smell of the sea. But I often saw him standing at the kitchen sink, absentmindedly catching and caressing the stream running from the faucet.

Nephews and nieces sat entranced by stories he told of fighting fires in the city. I remember Uncle Charlie bowing and shaking his head as he recalled families who sat weeping on curbs, tears soaking their nightclothes as the flames reflected in their eyes. The hoses, he said, nearly pulled his arms from their sockets. With reverence and fear, the fireman with the middle name of Blaise, praised the water for saving the city and cursed it for the icy nights and the flooded basements in which family treasures were drowned.

Pittsburgh's steel mills, working round the clock, kept the taverns open all night. When Charlie's mates headed off to douse their own fires with boilermakers, he took the trolley straight home. And through all the family weddings and wakes, we never saw him drink a drop.

Yet he drank himself to death.

When his eldest son married and moved to New England, he invited Charlie to his house near the beach. At first Charlie refused to visit, saying he had no interest in the beach. But when his first granddaughter was born, Charlie relented and traveled to Massachusetts, where he would once again encounter the sea.

Charlie was struck to his knees before the blue eyes of his granddaughter and the waves as they crashed against the seawall and retreated to the depths. Throwing his freckled arms toward the Atlantic, he couldn't bear to leave, as if the tide had seized him. He returned several times a year and always had to tear himself away, each time more painful than the last.

At home, he lined window sills and bookcases with shells and ordinary-looking rocks from the coast. He waxed about the mist and the kelp. And, even though he rarely swam and never set foot in a boat, if you got him started talking about the ocean, he blathered like an old salt on a barstool. My cousin and his wife had three more children, and Charlie visited more often. As much as the children, the sea itself drew him.

Finally, he couldn't leave it behind.

Take into account his cockeyed religious fervor, which leaned farther over the gunwales of his sanity as the years went on, convincing him that God had laid the Atlantic Ocean at his feet in a gesture of abundance. Charlie vowed to make it his own, to become one with it, to honor the Lord through gratitude.

He asked a buddy to steal two five-gallon carboys from the water coolers at city hall. And so the next time he and my aunt Dolores drove up to Massachusetts, Charlie loaded the empty bottles into the trunk of his car.

He waited until the last hours of their visit, then parked at the beach, waddled into the bay and allowed the surf to fill his bottles. He corked them, lugged them to the car, and turned his back on the ocean without regret this time, without so much as a glance in the rearview mirror.

Once home, he stashed the bottles in the closet near the front door. I had seen them one afternoon as I hung my coat, but couldn't guess why they were there. Every morning for two years, as the sun broke through the clotheslines in the backyard, while he waited for the kettle to whistle, he padded over to the closet with a juice glass in his hand and decanted a few ounces of brine.

He bragged about his regimen one Sunday evening during my family's regular visit. We had grown accustomed to Uncle Charlie retiring early on Sundays. When he was younger, he excused himself and went to bed. But as he grew older and more peculiar, he made a show of unfolding an old army cot in the living room and stretching out with the children as Disney's Tinkerbell appeared on the TV screen.

Dressed in his pajamas, he stood before us and announced: "I have found the essence of life, of us all, of eternal health!" He raised a glass of brackish water from the Massachusetts Bay, that very bay surrounding Boston Harbor, its effluent ripened in a dark closet on Pittsburgh's North Side. He praised God, his children, the earth and its waters, and tossed it back. "Down the hatch," he croaked, wiping his lips with the back of his hand.

We were aghast. Even I, an adventurous teenager and susceptible to any dare, could not imagine a wager high enough or a girl pretty enough to make me swallow the salty goo and tufts of algae I saw slide from the glass. Then Charles Blaise Cassidy lay down to sleep, all his blessings gathered around him and his faith taking him from within.

His wake was wet with reverence. But all I could think about were the legions of microbes, apparent in the green slime floating in his juice glass, attacking his organs, how water had delivered him to the new world, brought salvation to the victims he saved, called him home, and carried him away.

14

Popularity, Politics, and Patronage

As a Catholic boy, I felt like President Kennedy had been shot out from under me. When dressed in my Sunday best, I emulated his habit of walking with his hands in his pockets. I built a model of PT-109 and adored his wife and kids. His stated ideals and all the lessons I learned from priests, and scouting, and my parents' persistent volunteering, ignited in me a flame of service. As self-conscious as I was, the notion of coming to the rescue set fire to my ego.

By the time I reached junior high, a full blown Boy Scout, I saw helping as the daily work of heroes. The atmosphere in public school was charged with cliquishness, jealousy, and nastiness. The first time I witnessed a kid drop a tray in the lunchroom and heard the laughter and ridicule erupt from my peers, something the nuns would never have tolerated, I was struck by the cruelty and moved, without hesitation, to the site of the accident. I remember those scenes because they happened regularly. It could have easily been me. I admit that, after a while, I did think about how others saw me—squatting in an aisle with the embarrassed kid, cleaning up the mess and helping them carry it away—and probably took too much pride in my response. Sometimes I even watched for the shyest, clumsiest, or most bullied kids to slip up. The popular ones didn't need my help.

All my classmates in Catholic school would have done the same. But manners were rarer at the junior high and I invented a role for myself, a Boy Scout, a nice guy who stepped in when nearly everyone else was laughing, and carried that role as we all transferred to "the big house," —Ambridge High.

My older brother had taught me how to handle intimidation. Mark threatened, ridiculed, and tortured me relentlessly, and I gave it back. He proved that even tough-seeming guys were often, like him, pussycats beneath the bluster. If I let hooligans have a little fun before drawing the line and walking away, they would let up. Mark also challenged authority, making it easier for me to question the power of bullies. If I could get them talking, maybe make them laugh, I could get away with being a pacifist the bad guys didn't bother.

In the halls of Ambridge High School, massive football players walked like gunslingers, shooting gritty glances at greasers and motorheads, guys who wore torn shirts and denim jackets, carried chains and knives, and spent their days in the vocational shops. Half of these thugs grew up in the hills and farmland, on wooded lots strewn with decaying cars, guarded by angry dogs. The other half grew up on the streets of Ambridge, in its pool halls, housing projects, and insulated ethnic strongholds. The difference often bred violence.

Busty, Marlboro-smoking broads with a barnyard understanding of sex clung to the backwoods bullies. The downtown hoodlums were decorated with gum-cracking future mob princesses adept at shriveling penises with a single snarl.

In addition to having a brother who showed me the true nature of teenage badboys, I had a powerful family connection to keep me safe. Uncle John, Milt's brother and a former army sergeant, was the Electric Shop teacher in the basement. Down there, the ruffians who electrocuted each other for sport both loved and feared my uncle, who had a reputation for being reasonable, funny, and as tough as a Steelers lineman. So, unless one of the wiseguys wanted more trouble than he could handle, he considered my last name and gave me a wide berth.

As it turned out, I never explicitly sought my uncle's protection, but I did visit him and eat lunch with him and his charges now and then. I wanted to know the grittiest characters in the school, and keep peace with them. The political animal in me had begun to emerge.

In 1970, Vietnam dominated public discussion. The tumult of 1968, in particular, still reverberated through popular culture from civil rights to women's rights, through music, television, and movies. The word "revolution" came up more frequently, along with dreams of changing the world. But protests and sit-ins opposing the war or supporting civil rights made little noise in Ambridge, where the mills were feeding the war machine and the police ranks were strictly Caucasian.

I lay in my top bunk at home, surrounded by maps, reading Kerouac and Hesse, seeing Southeast Asia fester as a kind of wound, yearning to cross the oceans, or at least the country. But I had causes to support right here, where industries and unions held sway over workers who faced danger, drudgery, and daily doses of toxicity. Wages rose, but so did insecurity and pollution. Ironically, only war could give my neighbors peace of mind. We clung to the withering tendrils of a once-great industrial machine, and its life-support—defense contracts—were harvested by dirty, self-serving politicians, the same company yes-men, union bosses, washed-up athletes, and ambitious ninnies who started their careers courtesy of Merchant Street bookies and bankers investing in future favors. Patronage ate public services alive. Nobody got a job at the water authority, in the fire department, the county commissioners' office, or the town dump without a sponsor, to whom they owed at least fealty and, at most, regular cash "donations." One hot-bed of scandal, our local school board, was dominated by self-interested business people in construction and real estate. At one time, a new school had been erected on property sold to the district by the president of the board who brazenly built himself a big new house adjacent to the school, using the very same distinctive bricks. Everyone looked the other way, and anyone with the authority or temerity to investigate had already been paid off. Business as usual. And I, with my white-boy afro and insolent questions, hoped to undermine it.

The school board intended to raze the high school and replace it with what grumbling taxpayers and teachers called a Taj Mahal. Apparently the contractors and colluding board members had failed to adequately grease the machinery, and those left out of the chain of bribes spoke out, calling for a rare and often highly orchestrated public hearing. The do-nothing, do-everything argument had been polarized and nobody saw a third way. I leapt at the chance to write a killer paper for civics class.

Before what promised to be a hot hearing, I interviewed board members (two of whom had never finished high school) the superintendent (who brandished a fake PhD), townspeople, teachers, and students. When I stood to report my findings, as a representative of the high school's student council, the chairman invited me to the podium. I laid out a dozen of the most practical ideas in a short speech. After the third outburst of applause, I felt a rush of power and began counting the interruptions—eleven by the time I finished.

I had no idea. The meeting ended before I could gather

myself, and Charlie Laughlin, our state senator and the most influential man at the hearing, buttonholed me. Nobody knew where he stood on the project. He hadn't tipped his hand. I thought, Uh-oh, this guy is going to have my family's house torched. "Well done, son. That new building's D-O-A," he said, laughing, his smile as big as a billboard. "Do you have a job lined up for summer?"

"Um. I do," I said. I had been working for about a year as a car-hop at a drive-in restaurant. "But what do you have in mind?"

"How would you like to work in the Senate, as a page?"

"I think I'd like that very much," I said in disbelief.

"Good," he said, shaking my hand, "talk it over with your parents. You'll have to live in Harrisburg, but I'll help you out with that." He handed me his card, and I stared at the blue and gold seal of the Pennsylvania Senate. "Again, great speech. Call me soon," he urged.

As he shook my hand, he winked, probably an old habit, but it made me wince just a little, because it meant I now had a connection—the kind of currency that changed fortunes. I hadn't sought it but there it was, in a plaid sport coat, handing out favors.

15

Humility and Its Opposite

All four of my grandparents left Europe and arrived at the doors of their newly naturalized American relatives, only to run straight into the Great Depression, making them reflexively hospitable, frugal, and watchful for harder times. Their worries seemed quaint in the prosperous 1960s, but their children—our parents—knew how to live on very little.

Financial insecurity plays out in different ways. Steelworkers earned bigger incomes with every union contract, some bought new cars every two years, went farther afield for vacations, and expanded their houses. The class-anxious spent money on decoration, installing fountains and statuary (think *Manneken Pis*—the pissing boy—and cement lions) in their front yards. My family stuck to the old frugality: rebuilding our own transmissions, making our own wines, growing vegetables, fishing, and hunting—all for the freezer. We didn't eat the fish out of the polluted Ohio, but the extremely thrifty and poor, mostly black families, did. My father managed debt, paying it off and borrowing carefully, often in the face of layoffs and shutdowns.

For those who listened, the rumblings portending the collapse of the American steel industry began in the late 1950s, with steelmakers facing almost no competition and the demand for consumer goods on the rise. Profits climbed steadily and unions won ever-increasing wages for their members.

The Vietnam War kept our three biggest employers going: Jones & Laughlin Steel, American Bridge, and Armco Steel. Those of us who opposed that war in squeaky high school demonstrations did so at peril, because war meant jobs. When it was over, defense contracts dried up, sending a shockwave through industries that were paying single wage-earners enough to support a family of four. Something had to give. That's the way my father saw it.

During dinner-table conversations, Milt told us the structures he drew were being made from imported beams; he felt the pressure of tighter timetables and paranoid managerial tactics; and he whistled in disbelief when he sipped his coffee, lit a Viceroy, and announced, eyebrows raised, that the union scored another big pay increase for him and his fellow steelworkers. His Depression-born pragmatism made him distrust an unsustainable windfall and he explained why he sensed American Bridge and the whole steel industry crumbling. His hunches led him to bring home moonlight jobs he worked on in the basement, where he had converted the ping-pong table into a drafting setup. Inflation was driving up prices, and most evenings, he went downstairs in an effort to avoid disaster once the bridge company shut down.

I had been doing odd jobs around the neighborhood for pocket money since I was ten. At thirteen I started caddying at the country club a few miles away where I could hear golfers who were mostly mill foremen, executives, and gangsters refer to each other as assholes and whores while repeatedly calling me a dumb fuck. They treated caddies like slaves who worked for tips and the privilege of learning to play on Monday mornings. Carrying the bags taught me obedience, humility, and the differences between men when they are away from their families and often in competition: Some were cool, funny, and mannerly, others cheated, threw clubs, and behaved like animals.

But I hadn't truly tasted humiliation until, at fifteen, I took a job as a car hop at Big Boy's Eat 'n' Park, a local drive-in restaurant. The job sounded like fun to me and I leapt at the ad in the newspaper. Only two miles away, I hitchhiked to work and walked home. Somehow, I set aside my teenage self-consciousness when I suited-up for work, slipping into black-and-white-checked food service pants, a white short-sleeve shirt, non-slip shoes, and a paper hat that forced my curls out around my ears, much like Bozo the Clown. I helped the dishwasher, the porter, and the cooks. I cleaned the toilets and waited on customers—a few families but mostly joy-riders and hot-rodders who preferred sitting in their cars on a breezy evening, listening to their radios, snuggling with dates, waving to their friends, and flashing their parking lights at cars they wanted to race. Those would be the guys who amused their slutty girlfriends by ordering "furburgers" from me as I stood, pimply and clueless, with my order pad. In front of the restaurant stretched a wide, quarter-mile straightaway. At any point in the evening, after I unhooked the empty tray from the driver's side windows, I'd see a Camaro and a Mustang, let's say, rumble out of the lot. The other diners would turn down their radios and wait to hear screeching tires and boasting pipes, then stare toward Duss Avenue, looking for a flash of flying metal, setting off a thrill that buzzed through the lot until the victor rolled in with a fist raised high.

Eventually, I worked my way out from under the paper hat and into a hairnet as a short-order cook, a job that felt like destiny to me. My mother had already allowed me many adventures in the kitchen, cooking and baking, and I thrived on the camaraderie, speed, and precision of cooking for paying customers. Over the ensuing years I would work in several other restaurants, but my first year as a cook was golden, a combination I'd rarely find again—fellow cooks who were skilled, mellow, and mostly sober, a manager who was grateful for a good crew, and waitresses who pinched my cheeks, blew me kisses, and made me milkshakes to keep me going.

My tenure at the Big Boy was interrupted when I accepted the offer to work as a page in the capitol in Harrisburg, where I rented a room at the YMCA for the summer. I had my own room for the first time in my life—a humid cell with full bathroom down the hall. Clean towels, a single bed, a narrow wardrobe, a bureau, a tiny chair with a desk to match that was near enough to use as a nightstand, in which I found a shoelace, an empty condom wrapper, and an Alice Cooper tape. *"Schoooolˋs out for summer!"* I listened to it over and over. For entertainment, I had a bagful of novels, a cassette player, and a window that opened to the loud, noxious, but always fascinating Front Street.

Living alone allowed me to scour the streets every evening, drop into coffeehouses where I found musicians and poets, introduce myself at a friendly pool hall, and make some extra cash working at La Scala, the Italian restaurant across the street. Tommy, the owner, let me wash dishes and bus tables on Wednesday nights, and prepare food—roll meatballs, fry sausages, that kind of thing—on Thursday nights.

During the session, I perched on the stair of the Senate rostrum, dazed by the pontificating senators whose oratorical skills were no match for the priests in church. Once the budget session ended, most of the senators went home. A few stayed in town to party and fool around at the office. I stumbled upon them snuggling with their secretaries under the glossy portraits of their All-American families. A couple of these honorables dispatched me to the nearby Holiday Inn to deliver envelopes to "legislative assistants" who met me at the door wearing bathrobes, standing in bare feet with curlers in their hair, blushing.

A feeling of independence set up shop within me. Free from the familiarity of Ambridge, I could open a conversation with someone sitting next to me at a lunch counter without finding we were distant cousins, and walk away a stranger or a potential friend. My anonymity made me invisible and I felt as if I could go anywhere unnoticed. I learned a new job, and found my way around a new city. In the capitol's law library and state archives I rarely saw anyone else under thirty, and those I saw, I admired. I had the freedom I had always wanted. I knew it, as did my parents. I had become my own (impressionable, idealistic, and ambitious) man, as green as springtime.

At the end of the summer in Harrisburg, I toured the new US Steel Tower in Pittsburgh, the tallest skyscraper in the state. From the observation deck, I could look into Three Rivers Stadium, where the Pirates were defending their World Series title and the Steelers would begin their rise to prominence. I could see the sprawling Homestead Works, where the steel surrounding me had been cast, spewing fire and smoke, beginning to gasp for life, as the number of steelworkers fell for the first time in history, and would continue to slide until the global conglomerate that built and owned the floor beneath me would falter until losing ownership of the building itself.

The gathering storm eventually wiped out the region's employment base and triggered the largest exodus of workers the nation had ever seen. In the center of the impending storm, Pittsburghers were feeling prosperous and Bridgers were riding the wave, but a sense of foreboding also arrived, fueled by skepticism about the post-Vietnam economy, rising inflation, and preposterous steelworker wage increases. We didn't use the word "unsustainable" much back then, but the feeling was pervasive.

My stint as a page in the Pennsylvania State Senate during a time when the US Justice Department declared the state the most corrupt in the nation, turned me into a zealous young reformer. And my father's ominous observations of the steel industry fueled a sense of urgency in me, pushing for political, societal, and economic change. Woe to the high school administrators I harassed in the fall of 1971 as a high school junior and a smartass activist.

I campaigned for George McGovern, mediated racial conflicts in school, and hosted an event for Vietnam Veterans Against the War. I had shifted my heroic quest from entering the priesthood to entering politics. Any remaining notion to go to seminary and take the spiritual route toward justice faded behind my newfound fascination with the legal system, and disappeared entirely beneath the crushes I had on girls.

They all fascinated me. I was a virgin, but the notion of leading a celibate life became unthinkable. Italian girls captivated me. Croatian girls had a look I'd see in photos of Parisian women. And, while trying to understand my relationship with Mimi Lacarno, I took advantage of the town's diversity, dating a sweet Ukrainian, a stunning Pole, a translucent Swede, and the only Jewish girl in the school. She broke my heart when she caved to her mother's demand that she stop dating a Catholic. But I healed quickly and moved on.

As far as the average steelworker could tell, the mills were doing well, and the Vietnam War continued throughout that year; it was hard to estimate its effect on my classmates. The protests, the alienation of veterans, race riots, assassinations, and corrupt political leadership dragged an idealistic youth movement into apathy. My peers made me class president because nobody else wanted it.

After being introduced as a commencement speaker, I removed my mortar board on the way to the microphone, made a point of tucking away the approved speech, and extemporaneously addressed matters nobody spoke about in public—overt racism that divided the town, cronyism, and the rigid leaders of unions and mills who refused to look ahead. The speech easily went over the top. Parents squirmed in their seats. My classmates behind me supplied some applause but I felt uncomfortably alone, as if I had undressed in front of the entire town and exposed all my idealism and naiveté. I had. And I couldn't help it, because I had their attention and I was determined to try to make good use of it.

Had I been alert and self-aware enough, I might have noticed the trouble I had with taking too much license from my popularity, much like the public figures and authorities I called into account. In the years ahead, I would learn how seductive politics could be and how reckless I could feel with even the slightest amount of power in my hands.

Reflecting back on this time decades later, I asked my parents how they felt when I moved into the Harrisburg YMCA for the summer to take the job. "Your mother didn't like it much, but she got used to it. We knew you wanted to go places and do things. I told her, 'You don't have to worry about Paul; he's a good bullshitter.'"

I knew what he meant. But I didn't like hearing it.

"What? Did you think I was a liar, that I made up stories?"

"Yeah, you made up some stories. But, no, you didn't lie to us."

He was surprised that I took offense, knowing that I had heard it before, but not from him, not in a while anyway, so he wanted to explain. "You could talk. You talked your way into jobs. You talked your way out of fights. A lot of people think things, but can't say them. You could. That makes you a good bullshitter. What am I supposed to say? I just say you're a good bullshitter, and everybody knows what I mean. When people around here say that, they don't mean anything *bad* by it."

A few months earlier, a dear aunt paid me the same compliment. I was explaining how I found sources and arranged interviews for magazine stories. "You've always been such a good bullshitter!" she raved, in front of other women who smiled and nodded in agreement. After winning an award for a story I wrote, Betty said, "Well, you always did have the gift of gab."

I admit that I'm talkative and ready for discussion. I invite opinions and advance my own, sometimes when I hardly know what I'm talking about—an impulse that embarrasses me. That impulse, according to Professor Harry G. Frankfurt, who wrote the only definitive work to date, *On Bullshit*, leads to bullshitting. I am also guilty of exaggeration, hyperbole, and speaking without adequate reflection. But despite my reputation as a bullshitter in Ambridge, I try to avoid trading in falsehoods.

Although I respect the professor for his analysis, as far as it goes, his essay fails to take into account all the uses of the term as slang, applied differently up and down the socio-economic ladder, as well as its geographic variants. Let me try to say it plainly: What bullshit is to one is not bullshit to others. It does not necessarily stem from lying. Around Ambridge, bullshitting can be used interchangeably with talking, as in, "We missed the bus because we were busy bullshitting." It's akin to a "bull session" or "shooting the shit."

I first heard the word *bullshitting* applied to the men who, having escorted their families to Mass, stood outside Divine Redeemer, smoking and bullshitting. Never did I hear that they were talking or gabbing or even just hanging out. For a long time, I thought bullshitting could only be done outside a church.

The bullshitting I grew up with includes guessing, rationalizing, posing, embellishment, exaggeration, and, harmlessly enough, talking with a measure of eloquence. The laborers and factory workers, housewives and shopkeepers around Ambridge had little use for articulation or rhetoric. Many struggled to express themselves, and viewed elegance in communication as effete, elitist, hyper-educated and arrogant. In an effort to stave off inferiority, they lumped it in with bullshit. I saw it at local meetings where scholars and experts spoke about new programs in the schools, giving complex presentations. In the audience, eyes began to roll. The slightest confusion quickly gave way to boredom and mistrust. "So what do you think?" I'd ask the parents afterwards. "It just sounds like bullshit to me," most of them said.

This mistrust of intellectualism taught me to hold scholarship modestly. In a community that prized athletic achievement, simple living, family, and job security, there was a fear that academic excellence bred feelings of superiority. Kids who did well in school would abandon the community. The status conferred by academic degrees could raise suspicion and jealousy. In day-to-day living, budding intellectuals were encouraged to keep their accomplishments to themselves.

Sometimes I see the self-esteem movement of the 1980s as a backlash against the idea of building character through modesty. Take my sister Laurie, a brilliant student, whom my parents urged to remain silent about her test scores at the dinner table so she wouldn't embarrass the rest of us. When a friend, the oldest of five, won a college scholarship from the steel company where her father worked, he handed the notification back to her and said, "Way to go, Miss Lucky."

My talking, inquiring, speculating and analyzing have led me into a line of work unheard of among my family and peers in Ambridge. Growing up, I had never met a writer, a journalist or a poet. It never occurred to me that I could become one.

16

Sure But Not At All Certain

For all of my curiosity and desire to travel, the limitations of growing up near the edge of the Midwest meant that I turned eighteen and had yet to see the ocean. Late in the summer of 1973, my cousin Mike asked me to ride shotgun in his Austin Healy for a road trip and a week in Massachusetts. A few years earlier, his brother, Tom, had married Carol Antonucci in a big Italian wedding in Steubenville, Ohio, and their small family now lived in a beach town south of Boston. After thirteen hours of hard driving, the top down all the way, I began seeing gulls overhead. We turned off the four-lane and onto the shore road before dusk and I felt the temperature drop, moist air collecting in my hair, and smelled what could only have been marine life washing over the Healy's windshield and casting me into a dreamy dimension. I grabbed the top of the windshield and stood on the seat to peer over the seawall and catch my very first glimpse of the grey, green, and restless Atlantic.

Mike laughed and kept on laughing, perhaps remembering his first encounter with the ocean and thrilled he could bring me to this edge. We parked and walked out onto a jetty. Now I was surrounded by the sea and I felt as if I had passed into the afterlife. I wished I had, because, for the first time in my life I stood in a spot I wanted to remain in forever. Let life go on for others; I would have died for the simple privilege of staying put.

Mike fired up the Healy again and tore me away from my place in heaven, only to drive three short blocks to his brother's cottage. As we unpacked the tiny trunk, a tall, tanned goddess in cutoffs trotted barefoot across the lawn and threw her arms around Mike. He was surprised and I was stunned to see Liz, Carol's younger sister, who he hadn't known would also be staying for a week. She turned to me with a smile I could paint right at this moment, down to the shade of her lips and widening bottomless eyes. I had met her at Tom and Carol's wedding—the bridesmaid my mother teased me about once and later poked me for staring at. Soft-spoken and self-effacing, she made me want to know all about her. I wrote to her soon after the wedding, and she wrote back, sending me her senior picture. Like me, she also had wild, curly hair she tried to tame and straighten to fit the styles of the day. Our correspondence had ended after two letters, but here she was, welcoming us to the house.

Every morning just after sunrise, I would stroll out to the jetty where Liz would find me later. I peppered her with questions, wanting to know how she survived Catholic high school and why she had chosen Ohio University, where she'd be going at the end of the month. Together in the kitchen, cooking meals for the family, we slid around and behind each other in a kind of dance I've always enjoyed with helpers and fellow cooks. We babysat, and I wanted her to notice how much children liked me, even though I was impatient with them and wished they'd fall asleep so I could be alone with her. On the beach, she explained the tides and showed me where to find sand dollars. At night in the surf, she wowed me with the magic of bioluminescence. She was an enchanting teacher, and

I was supple in her hands, hands that held mine on long walks by the end of the week.

If Liz and I hadn't been starting college days later, we might have stayed in Massachusetts. We had begun to fall in love. At the time, though, I would never have admitted it, so determined was I to avoid love's traps and limitations, at least as I understood them. Yet it felt exactly the opposite: endless and unfolding, like the mysteries of the sea being revealed with each breaking wave. She satisfied my interest and piqued it again in the next moment. She possessed a quiet grace and a searching soul, one that clawed at the cage of conventionality. Her fingers probed the air or a tabletop for words that expressed her passions—mostly for the state of the world, children, health, and nature. Like most of the women I'd fallen for, conversation with Liz kept me on the edge of my seat and convinced me that women deserved more close attention than men. It sounds unfair, but it's proven mostly true for me over the decades. Liz, though, surrendered more than other women I'd known, more of her thoughts, feelings, and affections, making it so I could know her more quickly and I could trust her immediately. We promised to see each other as our lives opened a new chapter. She would be leaving her parents' home in gritty Steubenville for bucolic Athens, Ohio, and I was diving into the urban noise and concrete campus at the University of Pittsburgh.

During my first week in college, the atmosphere in the Oakland section of Pittsburgh and all the beautiful college women intoxicated me, and, smitten as I was with a new love-interest and attached as I might have been to my old girlfriend, I became a very distracted boy. I trusted my instincts and made impulsive choices. I woke up every day more fascinated by my surroundings and improvised from one moment to another. My father had left me at Pitt with two bits of advice: "Too much of anything is bad for you," and "There's no one woman in the world for you," a pearl Milt was qualified to deliver, having found my mother after tragically losing his young, first wife. His wisdom shaped my attitude, my avid desire to know as many women as possible. The legal drinking age had fallen to eighteen a year earlier, meaning I could blow money buying drinks for girls in bars. And, once I discovered sex, I began looking for it behind every smile and budding friendship. But I'm getting ahead of myself.

My first Saturday on campus—freshman orientation—I joined refrigerator-sized football recruits from my dorm on their way to Schenley Park for a free concert in a natural amphitheater. The skies looked threatening but I didn't care. I wanted to toss a ball around with the big boys and run barefoot on the lawn.

Only about fifty or so students were there, sitting on blankets or lying back, pointing at the clouds, checking each other out and tossing Frisbees while the band tuned up under a geodesic shell. Without preliminaries, the scruffy lead singer struck a hard rhythm line on his Fender and a beefy sax player caught our attention. Looking around, I didn't know a soul in this crowd, giving me a freedom I'd never felt before. By the end of the explosive opening number, we were astonished, facing the stage, and bopping with the music until the lead guitarist fell back and a bushy-bearded upperclassman stepped up to the mike. He told us he'd known these rockers from high school in New Jersey and they called themselves The E Street Band. Amid a smattering of applause, mostly from a clot of kids from Philly, Bruce Springsteen rushed the mike and launched into "Rosalita."

Hooked, I waded into the crowd and, tentatively at first, started dancing with barefoot strangers. Soon, the skies darkened, the clouds opened, nobody ran for cover, the band didn't let up, and we kept dancing until sunshine broke over us. I remember steam rising from our bodies and a huge whoop that went up when young, scrawny Springsteen pointed to the top of the hill, where a rainbow reached across the sky.

As would be true for millions more, his odes and beats and throaty stories found their way into my heart. I wanted to go into the streets. I wanted to see the boardwalk and boulevards for myself. And most of the kids with whom I was soaked to the bone were summer boardwalk boys and girls, lots of Jewish girls, their mothers nowhere in sight—a radical break from the Catholic girls I'd grown up with. Only days later I tried to lose my virginity, but it would be weeks before two women, wide-eyed at my admission, simultaneously engulfed me in a trundle bed and giggled their way through my first experience. I know what it sounds like, but it was a slippery, dark, and disorienting blur of tickles, wiggles, and hair, I not knowing which, or where, or what was going on, but we all had fun, though I felt like something of an accessory. That discovery still awaited me, though, on that rainy afternoon in 1973, when, under Springsteen's spell, I enlisted as a soldier in the sexual revolution.

My roommate had different ideas. I knew I was about to meet someone unlike anyone I'd met before when I saw his own hand-drawn portrait of Mahatma Gandhi above his bed. He had already created a tidy and soulful space—books on the shelves, sheets on the bed, a guitar case propped in the corner. Tom Waseleski's father had died when he was a boy, making him the man of the house, comfortable with responsibility from an early age. Though serious and studious, he smiled warmly when I met him and showed a durable sense of humor throughout a year that must have been irritating for him—

disgusting from time to time.

Tom's girlfriend Saundy—a pretty, sweet, easy-going scholar who had known Tom since high school—came over to study with him nearly every night. She had an unforgettable laugh set on a hair-trigger. They drank tea and tried to concentrate while I cracked wise to hear her giggle, and hammered at a typewriter before drinking buddies and waifish poets banged on the door and took me away. Some nights, Tom sat at his desk and wrote music, picking notes out of a guitar one at a time and jotting them down. I cleaned flasks, carboys, and airlocks as part of a winemaking enterprise Vito Zingarelli and I had bubbling in our closets. Tom and I sketched with charcoal, wrote and read poetry, and discussed politics. And, while Tom walked Saundy back to Carlow College, a Catholic girls' school nearby, I pretended sophistication with girls upstairs, sipping homemade Lambrusco and fumbling with their anatomy.

At my worst, I stumbled in drunk with a nursing student and we made love in my bunk, four inches away from Tom's. I apologized the following day. He insisted he was sleeping, and never mentioned it again. *Mensch*—the hung-over girl called him.

I'm not sure why, but Tom and I had signed up for an educational experiment concocted by some of the top professors in the arts and sciences. They designed a freshman program they called The Alternative Curriculum, intended to upend the rigidity of the freshman experience and give a small group of students a chance to work in close collaboration with the faculty. We both chose to write poetry with Ed Ochester, a generous man who made poetry personal for me and countless others, and has become a celebrated poet. I also conducted anthropological research, observing the behavior of orangutans at the zoo a few days a week. Overall, I dabbled—in art, philosophy, literature, and history—all of which suited my nature but left me rudderless for the subsequent three years, unassigned to an advisor and left to figure out how I could assemble a transcript that would help me enter law school.

The program, though, gave me time to dive into all the cultural, and free, events happening around. I could look at modern art for hours, and crashed the opening of the Carnegie Museum's Scaife Gallery. The college's studio theater put me in the center of experimental productions. But music, especially live music, took me where no other art form could. I bought student tickets for matinees—symphony, ballet, opera—in the concert halls downtown. Always on Sunday afternoons. Sometimes I'd find a date, but was happy to go alone.

Friends opened stage doors and back rooms; I could hang out in the shadows while Tom Waits and B. B. King, Chuck Berry and Willie Dixon, tuned up. Pitt and Carnegie-Mellon share a section of the city that was dotted with low-profile, intimate jazz clubs and I found my way to them and learned to sip drinks slowly for the privilege of staying. I volunteered at the annual jazz festival in my sophomore year and every year thereafter. A craving for more chases and bop sent me into the streets and smoky clubs, where only respectful students ventured.

One club tempted me every time I passed it on the way home to my apartment. A blind saxophone impresario named Eric Kloss led the house band at Sunny Daye's Stage Door, where an older crowd of well-dressed men and women, black and white, spoke in soft tones and showed an easy intimacy. I sat in the same seat, in the corner, against a wall, and spent money on drinks I couldn't afford. It became like a church to me, where the music made sense in that it traveled from one note to the next seemingly without a plan, taking me with it from moment to moment, suspending my ambitions and allowing me to dream of going where life took me.

My work-study job, though, kept me out of the clubs most nights and saved me from going broke. From 10:00 p.m. until 6:00 a.m., I sat at the entrance to campus buildings that were open all night—the dental school or the engineering building, for instance—checking in late-night visitors. Most often I was stationed at the epicenter of campus, inside its architectural focal point. Approaching Pitt from just about anywhere, it's impossible to miss the modestly named Cathedral of Learning. At forty-two stories, this Gothic tower, made of Indiana limestone (the same as my revered library in Ambridge), dominates the landscape. Its Commons Room, the entire ground floor, covers a half-acre and has the proportions and conveys the feeling of a cathedral with arches vaulting three stories high. Surrounding the Commons Room are twenty-six classrooms, each styled after a classroom from another nation. The desks, seminar tables, chairs, stained glass windows, and wall panels were either imported through the largess of industrialists or donated as a cultural artifact by the nations themselves.

The entire Cathedral fell under my supervision from midnight until morning. I gave the thumbs-up to a passing patrolman twice a night and then went back to shuffling along the slate floor, my head bent to the essays of Michel de Montaigne.

I liked that Montaigne, a lawyer and magistrate in the late 1500s, had given it all up to examine himself and write what he discovered as he went along. He could be ruminative or controversial, willing to lob fire-bombs at the dogma of his day, while continually questioning and contradicting himself. The more exposure I had to literature and the arts, the more I doubted my teenage certainty and assertions, allowing Montaigne's pattern of thought to resonate with me. Throughout those long nights, I allowed Montaigne to inhabit me, imagining myself in his stone tower in Bordeaux.

Closing a compact edition of his *Essais* around one finger that marked my selected passage, I assumed the lectern in the English classroom, with its stained glass windows and oak furniture, or I situated myself on the pillows around an ebony table in the Japanese classroom to read aloud. Montaigne did all the talking, leading the imaginary students through what Graham Greene called "the divagations of the mind." Montaigne sought to prove nothing but an understanding of himself, and his train of thought meandered through the countryside, not like a Swiss express with an ambitious schedule, but more like a tourist coach of ideas and reasoning, clattering to the rhythm of the rails, throwing switches and likely to go anywhere.

How kind he was, I remember thinking, to let me in on his thoughts. A man four hundred years gone, who matched the music and the noise of my own thoughts, improvising melodies and philosophical riffs, like Sonny Rollins picking out a solo and floating it across the floor. I felt as if he played only for me, but I knew my audience could understand him, too. I became convinced that the folks back home, the ones who usually read no more than the box scores and the obituaries, could relate to Montaigne's introspection and misgivings.

He made perfect sense, running in one direction then wandering off in another—patterns of thought we all know. Through him, I recognized the ambler within me, who discovers where he is going by where he has gone. It reminded me of the attraction I felt for cowboy life, back when I strapped on plastic six-shooters, and rode the range of my imagination.

For the first time, I felt reassurance for having a nature I saw as anti-systematic. Montaigne saw himself as an "accidental philosopher." He loved the transitory, without constructions, models, and logical systems. He showed me that it might be okay to leave deduction and induction to scientists and lawyers. Reading him, I wanted to push aside professional advocates and fall in with the idlers Robert Louis Stevenson said "have a great and cool allowance for all sorts of people and opinions." That felt right for the times, and it felt right for me—much better than charging down narrow corridors of advocacy.

Montaigne made me want to embrace open questioning, to loosen the laces on corseted ideas, including my own. In trying to consider all sides, I feared losing my convictions and principles. Writers, philosophers, and especially lawyers must plant their feet on prescribed territory and defend it. Slowly, though, I began to see contradiction as a more natural state for me.

Logic and analysis helped me make decisions, but contradiction—advancing an idea, turning against it, doubting my doubt—made me feel alive, as if I had quietly picked a lock or blown a door off its hinges, leaving a gaping portal between what I had intended and what might happen. Whether I was falling into a jazz-induced trance or the admissions of Montaigne, what would it mean to resist my long-held ambitions, or at least question them? Was I desperate to get ahead or get away, devoting myself to cheesy desires: chasing status and girls? Why were saxophones and an ancient Frenchman seducing me with the beauty of changing my mind?

After my shift, I would walk through the early morning streets toward home, and I could hear the air horns call the shift change across the river in Homestead. I wished

PAUL HERTNEKY

every steelworker there could have been with me in those classrooms overnight. If we opened our minds and considered new choices, though, what would we choose? Later, when the steel industry fell, everyone in these valleys would confront that situation. Until then most would, by necessity, ignore the inevitable. Like me, they had no Plan B.

I couldn't imagine a change of heart when it came to my future. So I denied the doubts Montaigne raised within me. He would have approved of my refusal to swallow his attitudes whole, massive skeptic that he was. Instead, I reasoned that I could wedge his wisdom into ambition to bring the powerful and corrupt to their knees (and win admirers along the way). Shoving my improvisational nature aside, I sat on my imagination and held fast to my hero fantasy.

152

17

Curiosity as Curse

Improvising my way through college, I walked a wobbly line, bucking power and falling back on familiar rituals. Aspiring law students like me joined the Pitt Tenant Union, a campus organization that helped students understand leases and exercise their rights as tenants. Many of the volunteers also worked for a sister organization that, for the most part, sent advocates to night court to help students who had been arrested on misdemeanors arrange bail and avoid a frightening night in jail.

Wanting every chance to strike a blow for justice, I joined both groups. The Watergate scandal only deepened my commitment to practice law, battle the rotten establishment, and help the little guy and the disenfranchised. My overall skepticism extended to Catholicism, but the Church had yet to become a prime example of institutional crime and I still loved the symbolic hocus-pocus the Mass inspired in me as a kid. When it came to self-flagellation and sorrow, no day at church could beat Good Friday. After three grueling hours lamenting the supreme sacrifice of the ultimate hero, we took Jesus off the cross and went out for fried fish. Once each year, my parents treated the family to a real restaurant.

Stubby's stood near the town hall on Merchant Street, and its proprietor, Roy Stubbins, worked the levers of the Democratic

Party from his seat on the town's governing body. It had the look of a posh joint, an art-deco logo, and a curved façade of shiny black tile and glass block. My father held open the door to a barroom straight out of a gangster movie, its upholstered stools facing a carved mahogany back-bar and laced with the rich scent of cigars, aftershave, and fried haddock.

At four o'clock in the afternoon, the bartender greeted us and shook my father's hand while our eyes adjusted to the interior, dimly lit by globes hanging from the ceiling that were identical to the ones in the police station—no mere coincidence. We scooted into high-backed booths that lined the walls, each with its own jukebox directory, the kind of private eating chambers perfect for mob meetings and assignations. Farther back, alongside the kitchen, were rooms I never saw. Like most bars in Ambridge, that's where regulars played cards or dice, or where the bookies set up shop. Who knows what deals were cut in Stubby's? Everybody knew it was the true seat of power.

Nothing changed in Ambridge unless the bigshots, the party bosses, and racketeers worked it out. From their company offices and union posts, they ran the mills. From their seats on the borough council, they influenced police protection, commercial activity, and the public schools. Their tax schemes held sway in county government. And through it all, they set up loyal soldiers with lifetime employment in a place where a job meant survival. As a result, the wheels of the political machine turned slowly, grinding up dissenters and elevating virtual idiots to public office via obedient, straight-ticket voters.

In trying to understand the culture and politics of Ambridge—rigidity, influence-peddling, suspicion of change and new ideas, aging industries, and calcified unions—I needed only to look upriver to Pittsburgh. Institutions held power by supporting the status quo, discouraging hard-working people from moving up or away. I'd hear loyalty like this: "Hey, the bar mill's been good to me. Twenty years it's been payin' my bills and keepin' my kids in clothes." But it wasn't the bar mill, it was *you* who paid those bills and bought those clothes. "Yeah, well, I ain't complainin."

We were taught to know our place, feel lucky we had a job and keep on working. "Who do you think you are?" squelched talk of dreams and high-minded ambitions, spoken by those who had acquiesced and, for self-preservation, insisted you do the same.

"Curiosity killed the cat," my mother said in the car on the way home from church one Sunday morning. I immediately objected. I was only seven years old ("the age of reason" the church called it, making you ready to confess your measly sins and take communion), standing behind the front seat and leaning into the space between my parents, quizzing them about something the priest said. Betty's admonition wounded me and succeeded in shutting me up for a moment while I reflected. Curiosity was my favorite companion. Maybe it took only one of a cat's nine lives. Still, "How could it hurt anyone?" I asked.

"Sometimes you're better off not knowing," she said.

"But how do you know it's one of those times if you don't ask?"

She sighed and my father whistled a nonsense tune—his way of biting his tongue.

"Just be careful," Betty said, exasperated.

Ironically, Betty patiently listened for hours to her friends' troubles, asking careful questions and showing interest, earning her a reputation as a helpful sounding board, an avid practitioner of empathetic curiosity. Milt tried to take life at face value but he couldn't suppress his fascination with nature, people, and how things worked, obsessing over problems and learning new skills—driven by epistemic curiosity. They didn't recognize it, but their freedom of thought—puzzling and guessing, analyzing and innovating—saved me from the pessimism and disparagement of ideas I would hear outside the house, most tragically from teachers.

One of the great triumphs in the American scene since 2000 has been the rise of Pittsburgh as a vital city, reshaped by new industries and creative capital. Its reemergence largely comes from the thud of the region's economy hitting bottom in the early 1980s. Most of the mill towns outside the city, though, still plagued by cultural narrowness and mistrust of new ideas, and still burdened by anemic industrial bases and tax revenues, have yet to get off their knees.

The image of Pittsburghers (and Bridgers, by extension) as tough, unyielding, hard-drinking, and provincial, endures as a result of its industrial roots. Social scientist John Ingham studied the businessmen and the manufacturing landscape around Pittsburgh from 1870 to 1960. He says that Pittsburgh's iron and steel-producing families ran their mills like small and personal businesses that emphasized "success and control on the local scene, and they innovated just enough to maintain that control." They stayed small and resisted modernization to keep their status and their economic, social, and political influence over their businesses and the city.

When Andrew Carnegie moved into other industrial centers in Pennsylvania, Ohio, and Indiana in the 1870s, he brought modern Bessemer technology and high output. Small manufacturers either sold their antiquated plants to him or closed. Not in Pittsburgh, though, where the baronial families had no interest in losing their authority and sitting on the sidelines as investors and relics of an obsolete royalty with no power. Faced with extinction, they set forth a plan that "cautiously pursued innovation to achieve a profoundly conservative end: the continuity of their power and influence in the affairs of Pittsburgh."

Refusing to compete with Carnegie and US Steel, the families scaled back and made products for niche markets such as rail cars, industrial abrasives and the electrical equipment developed by George Westinghouse. This shift made the family operations highly profitable and preserved their place in the local aristocracy. They formed enclaves in outlying boroughs like Fox Chapel, Upper St. Clair, Mt. Lebanon, and the Ambridge neighbor, Sewickley.

Well into the twentieth century, these families forged marital alliances, bolstering their control of the local financial and banking scene. Upper-class paternalism set the tone not only in the mills, but nearly everywhere else. The moguls held their place, the managers found their place, and the workers knew their place. Each class went to different churches and schools, belonged to different clubs and shopped in different stores. Owners and managers took pride in this structure and assumed it functioned well for everyone, but workers found it hard to swallow without the help of whiskey.

Generations would erode the structure but not the culture. Because the mill-owning families cared more about maintaining their status than increasing their profits, they settled for the coziness of their local tribe instead of attaching themselves to the East Coast metropolitan class. Although they sent their sons to Ivy League schools, they expected them to return, take their place in the business, and spawn a new generation of executives and debutantes.

But the baby boomers developed broader interests than their parents, and fewer sons and daughters returned to the steelmaking valleys. Those who did return struggled to keep the family mills alive in the face of global competition, or they eventually threw in the towel and made their investments elsewhere.

Rich or poor, we all shared the same hookah—the smokestacks—and whether we rigged the meritocracy game or beat down a bright idea in the back room at Stubby's, we mirrored each other's movements. Both the owners *and* the laborers wanted to hold onto what they had—their place, their community, loved-ones, and family—despite the danger of having it all collapse.

Rise and fall, the reminders surrounded me even as I followed my parents and siblings into Stubby's. The once dominant steel industry now sagged under the weight of greed, globalism, and modernity.

Part of the thrill of Stubby's came from having endured three hours of services, kneeling before a realistic corpse of the crucified Jesus, giving me my first real sense of sadness. Before I had buried pet turtles and the baby bunny I found mauled by a cat, I took on the grief of losing the *Son of Almighty God*. The whole ordeal also attached "passion" to sacrifice. Who knew what to make of that?

As an altar boy during that intentionally painful ritual, I used a stiff linen cloth to wipe spittle off the Jesus figure's feet that each member of congregation kissed. Kiss, wipe, kiss, wipe, kiss, wipe. Between noon and three o'clock, with nearly everyone in town stuffed into churches, sucking incense and beating their breasts, a communal somberness chased the cars and pedestrians away from Merchant Street. Together, we celebrated sorrow, paddled boats we dared not rock, kissed the feet of the powerful; then we dove into a bar for doo-wop on the jukebox and pitchers of Iron City.

Stubby's fried fish kicked off another once-a-year holiday menu. Saturday's dinner had the feel of a picnic—colored hard boiled eggs were nestled into a large basket with a ball of sweet egg curd that had the look of cheese but the taste of dessert, a length of kielbasa from a local smokehouse, and rounds of *paska*, a handmade bread made only for Easter. We took the basket of delicacies to church on Saturday afternoon to be blessed and the meal had to be consumed that evening, a nod to the Passover Seder.

Chocolate bunnies appeared on Sunday, made at Andersen's Chocolate on Merchant Street, adjacent to a German bakery, where my girlfriend, Mimi, worked behind the counter. Finding her there suited the casual way I conducted my relationship with her. She lit up when I popped in and we would have a chat or make a date to see each other later. I always had fun on dates with Mimi. She was a smart conversationalist, a happy hand-holder, enthralling to look at, and ready to laugh. She gladly went just about anywhere, other than into sexual territory, but that set up a tension I thought one day would suddenly snap and make it worth the wait. Until then, we would talk for hours on walks or at dinner, go for drives and to movies and then we'd go back to her house, where her mother would feed me.

Mimi shared little of my frustration with life in Ambridge. She wanted to get away after high school, but hoped to return and live near her family, and she had no delusions about changing the world around her. Instead, she would find a career where she could improve the lives of one person at a time. How sensible. She would listen patiently to my fantasies about living in faraway places, following my nose wherever it took me and she must have wondered how she could fit into those plans. Either that, or she was just letting me talk, knowing that she would never separate me from my curiosity, wise enough to recognize its force.

18

Light and Nature

Happy in the green Hocking River valley around Ohio University, Liz Antonucci sent me beautiful letters in her decorative hand, full of news and poetry recalling our romance at the beach, and I sent her drawings and lyrics to love songs. She had become a vegetarian and introduced me to hand-lettered cookbooks filled with recipes for cheesy bean dishes, wiggly tofu, and whole wheat bread sturdy enough to shingle a barn. I played along; I'd do anything to be with her.

When I visited Liz in Athens, we spent most of our time outdoors, where she seemed propelled by breezes and softened by sun. Natural elements took possession of her and, within the reach of music, she seemed to rise straight out of the pitiless world. I had never encountered a spirit like hers, and she was mostly spirit. I could feel it and I loved it. But I was afraid to say so.

For me, her essence was also fused with that of the sea, since she had been near me during my first encounters with it. At my cousin's house in Brant Rock, Massachusetts, a squat two-bedroom cottage clad in weathered shingles and blue trim, sitting on a quiet corner just three blocks from the Atlantic, Liz slept on a mattress in the attic while I crashed in the unused dining room. I ached to sneak up to that attic. With no hallways, every room emptied into the ten-by-ten-foot living room, and the attic stairs pulled out of the ceiling near the middle of the room. At the time, Carol and Tom had three daughters, all under the age of six. One was an infant and I admired the ease with which Liz handled her. I was struck by the attention she devoted to everything she did, from drawing pictures with kids at the kitchen table to sautéing zucchini, from listening to my cockamamie theories about "dharma bums," to yanking every last weed from the garden. She poured herself into her task or conversation. When she disengaged, she could sit quietly forever with nothing but the wind to accompany her.

I have always loved the hour before dawn, and, continuing our pattern from the previous year, I brewed coffee and carried it, a book, and a notebook to the beach and found a comfortable seat at the end of the jetty to wait for sunrise. And her. We found very little time to be alone. If I waited and read for long enough she would come to find me. What a test of patience. Anticipation shattered my focus, and I often closed the book and let romance perform barrel rolls—*she loves me, she loves me not, here we are at the edge of the continent, ready to go anywhere, and will she go with me.*

As the sun climbed, and I all but gave up hope, she appeared, clutching a rolled towel and picking her way along the jetty, her eyes fixed on the tricky footing and one hand holding back her long, wild hair.

"Waiting for me?" she asked, finding a place to sit and dangle her tan legs off the rocks.

"Just reading," I lied, wanting to project a coolness she didn't buy, and then just feeling stupid.

"What did I miss?"

"About fifty feet of tide."

"Have you been swimming?" she asked, picking up a snail

shell and flicking it at my head. I had a tenuous relationship with water, scared to death of it as a kid, perennially unable to master the art of kicking or floating. I took enough swimming lessons to know how to frantically stay alive in deep water, and even then, for maybe only twenty minutes.

She wore a flowered orange two-piece, almost a bikini, under her cutoffs and t-shirt. She stepped out of her sandals and nudged a rolled towel with one of her perfect feet, unfurling my swim trunks, still damp from the clothesline where she had found them.

Liz swam like a porpoise, all around me as I floated like a long white ship at anchor.

Some mornings we'd sit back-to-back on the rocks and read until children and anglers encroached, walk the beach until we were sweating and ready to swim, or go into town for breakfast. We were living in a world of our own, and I lost myself in it.

"What if we stayed?" I asked her once.

"It's too crowded, too much pavement. Nice to visit, but I like the country."

Too much pavement? I lived in a city, and I hardly noticed the beach town's streets and crowds; plus, it all ended at the seawall where the ocean and the endless horizon presented a wide open world. The possibilities took my breath away though I couldn't figure out how they might unfold. I wanted Liz to help me visualize an adventurous future, but as we both headed inland, I left the beach behind and dismissed its effect as unreal.

I tried to keep a distance from her because I knew how strongly I felt, and I couldn't see how she fit into my plans. During my second visit to Athens, we scrambled along the banks of the Hocking River, and then sat in the tall grass above it. That misty Saturday morning, the colors bleeding into each other, seemed like an odd time and place to notice contrasts. We had known each other for two years by then and I always felt more in tune with her during silences that punctuated hungry make-out sessions. She lay back, her arms stretched above her head, enthralled and enchanted by the clouds, while I sat forward, my elbows on my knees, gnawing the juicy end of wild oat, feeling entirely at home in the setting, yet a little restless. I knew the woods and streams and fields—had run through them all my life, camping, picking berries, shooting animals, waking up with a face full of dew. She knew Steubenville—her father's novelty store, her uncle's sausage-making operation, the streets and barbershops frequented by Dean Martin. She had fallen for the natural world while I was infatuated with the city.

When I stayed at her family's house, her parents enveloped me in the kind of warmth I had felt from Mimi's parents and siblings. And their food, like that of Mimi's *famiglia*, cast a spell. I woke up to a kitchen table filled with nests of fresh pasta that would eventually join sausages in marinara sauce on my dinner plate. How could I resist marrying into such a family?

But at school, I drew a curtain behind me, resuming my ride on a torrent of sexual adventuring that I may have justified by reading *Tropic of Cancer* too many times. Through classes and politics, through parties and my three Philadelphian roommates, I met brainy girls and wild girls, nurses and painters, fellow budding lawyers and furry feminists. Skinny and awkward compared to my smooth-talking roommates, I stood aside and asked the girls questions about themselves, showing a willingness to become a friend, first. Betty taught me to listen, show interest and compassion, and anything could happen.

During my college summers, my job on a road crew that traveled the state kept me away from Mimi and Liz. When I had time off, I'd see one, then the other. My conscience nagged me for juggling the affections of these girls, keeping them secret from each other and occasionally lying to them. On top of that, when I had a chance to have recreational sex with other women, I took it, justifying my recklessness by refraining from making love with the two women who meant the most to me.

Somehow, that made all the philandering okay. Mimi knew of my escapades but never showed enough interest in sex to discourage me. Liz, however, made her desires plain, but with the forces of the moon and tides coursing through her and her countercultural aversion to unnatural birth control, I turned away out of fear of getting her pregnant and falling in love, mutually and exclusively. She had too much power over me, and I knew it while I watched her braiding her hair, barrette in her teeth, her fingers working with the same instinct with which she painted Peter Max-like scenes on her dormitory walls. Agile and artistic, her fingers waited patiently to help her make a point, to plant a seed or set out a line of calligraphy. Along with her eyes and lips, her walk and laugh, her hands portrayed an image of promise, fecundity, and terrifying fertility. If we made love, I would have to welcome full responsibility, not only for her heart, but for the baby we were bound to create.

But a girl can only be so patient, and she wanted to have some fun. I couldn't. Sex, for me, had to remain meaningless.

I feared very little back then, but I did worry about getting girls pregnant. My life would change instantly and I feared being trapped, stuck, and having all my dreams die. I knew the restriction of tight communities. More than anything, I needed freedom to improvise.

19

More Snoop Than Solicitor

I was a man on a mission, two missions, really: one to become a savior and hero, and the other to simply get away from everything I thought I knew. My family would do fine without me around and I needed some distance from all the birthdays, confirmations, weddings, christenings, graduations, and holidays. I knew that my friends would always be in my sphere, regardless of where we traveled. As for the savior business, the hero's quest to make a difference continued to drive me, lodged in my psyche after those long masses at Divine Redeemer, where I prayed to hear a calling from God. In lieu of that, I heard my own boyish desire, right out of a comic book. Without the hero's script I would be ordinary, and I didn't like the way that looked at all.

When I felt like I was losing my way, I hid in a jazz club or the stacks in the Carnegie Institute library, closed my eyes and tried to dream up a new vision that would make me something other than a milltown kid. I wanted to go where Ambridge couldn't be detected in my diction, like garlic on my breath, where I could present a clean slate to those I encountered, and to whom I was drawn.

None of my friends shared the fantasy of fleeing with me. Liz understood but also embraced practicality: graduating, getting a job, and settling down near home.

With the oil industry booming, and Armco Steel making pipe, Ambridge presented practical opportunities. Between my sophomore and junior year, when summer came again, I applied to work in the mills. They didn't call, so I went to work as an intern for a local attorney at minimum wage while doing research and studying for law school entry exams.

As much as I wanted to move beyond Ambridge, I cared about it. Like the girls I couldn't bring myself to say I loved, curiosity stood in the way of committing myself to it, yet my circle of family and friends made me feel loved. In return, I wanted to make myself useful there. Every day, I put on a suit and tie and dredged up legal precedents, ate lunch at my desk, and examined the depositions of accident victims while my boss paid the bills with real estate transfers and probate cases, divorces and wills. I began to see the way the money flowed through town and how landowners used the courts to circumvent local ordinances. I noticed how the mills danced around new clean air and clean water regulations. They had been polluting with impunity for decades and were now being asked to account for it.

My boss's skill as a trial lawyer disappointed me as well as his prison-bound defendants. He picked up steady work as a sort of magistrate for a juvenile detention facility. I helped review the cases, and one day I watched in horror as he badgered a child into tears so intense and sobs so deep as to burst the capillaries in her nose. Her mother sat stonily by as the girl filled her cupped hands with tears and blood, begging forgiveness. But "justice" sent her back to her cell.

By the time I filed into the auditorium at Pitt for my law boards, I had traveled nearly every road in the western half of the state. I had crossed all the rivers, seen most of the mills, met dozens of lawmakers, judges, mayors, and businessmen.

My dream of becoming a hero from the pulpit evolved into becoming a hero in court, but along the way, that dream had suffered from repeated awakenings. As a page, I saw powerful state senators behaving like bullies; I stewed while slumlords wriggled away from court orders; I twitched every time drug dealers made bail; I nodded off at the sheer boredom of daily life in a law firm; and I shuddered at the leaden digits on my tuition loan statements. In the end, I hoped that good scores on the exams would give me a boost, and a high-paying mill job in the summer before my senior year might help ease the worry.

My hands shook when I opened the envelope with my scores on the law boards. They were fine, good enough to get me into a school. I blew out one mighty sigh of relief, and immediately, when I tried to breathe again, felt smothered by anxiety. The idea of committing to another three years of studying much harder than I had been studying terrified me. But I had no other plan.

Doing well on the boards deserved celebration, though, and in a drunken lather, Jack Haight, another aspiring lawyer, and I cooked up an idea for an independent study in civil and criminal investigation. We were both English majors and we convinced the university to approve a nine-credit research project. We served half of our time with the detectives on the campus police, and the other half helping indigent clients of Legal Aid.

Articulate and nimble-minded, Jack had little tolerance for bullshit but lots of interest in having fun in an arch, subversive way. We once used the composite sketch kit to post pictures of undercover agents. When the campus police chief noticed these composites in our student offices, he knew it was our work, shook his head, and pretended to slap us on the wrists.

Most of our work through Legal Aid reminded me of why I wanted to become a lawyer. We fought slumlords who cheated our clients out of heat and hot water, and we hounded their lawyers into cooperating. We took down the mastermind of an apartment-finding scam who collected fees in the high season, disappeared, and reappeared in parts of the city where he found new prey, usually students.

I loved collecting evidence, research, interviews, and snooping around, and I wondered if I might be better suited to police work or to freelance investigations. Rifling through files and evidence, examining police reports, and burying myself in case law made me feel as if I had been set on fire, so flammable was my curiosity when looking for a break, a new angle, a discovery that would prove innocence, complicity, or guilt. I had never been a fan of mystery or crime stories. I thought private eyes were sleazy and cartoonish until I met a couple of them: former cops who had trouble with authority, or unfinished lawyers with drinking problems. They were townies, too, local guys working their home turf with a pocketful of contacts in the underworld. That wasn't me. I loved the work, but as an investigator, all I had was optimism, energy, and my congenital nosiness.

Jack brought street smarts and brashness to the investigative work. Hunter Thompson set the tone for him. We competed for how many documents we could read upside down on someone's desk. When we encountered unwilling sources, Jack was fond of moseying around the subject's desk, placing a hand on his shoulder and saying, "You might as well tell us; we're going to find out anyway."

As interns with the campus detective squad, we were playing the Hardy Boys meet Woodward and Bernstein. Thank God we were assigned to Ralph Lanier, who had every reason to lock us in the file room and keep us off the streets. But Lanier, a graying lieutenant who wore tweed jackets, and who lived his entire life in the Hill District, the city's largest black neighborhood, found us amusing. On our first day, he swiveled his chair away from his desk while snatching a pile of folders, stacking them on his lap and pushing his bifocals up to the bridge of his nose.

"Let's see, gentlemen, we got all kinds of bad actors on the loose. Most of them aren't dangerous, we don't think. And they figure we gave up chasing them. We got robbers, muggers, sexual deviants, and con men. Take your pick. You like stakeouts?"

"Sure!" I said, as Jack elbowed me but I didn't know why. It was January, that's why. For two months we stood in cold shadows in the middle of the night, waiting for an elusive suspect to visit his girlfriend, or mom, or partner in crime, then called in the patrolmen for an arrest. After proving ourselves through surveillance, Lanier promised we'd have a case we could really investigate.

One afternoon we got a report that several cadavers, human heads to be exact, had gone missing from the pathology lab in the dental school. Jack and I could finally visit the treasury of nitrous oxide tanks that made their way to campus parties. Our friends thought it festive to fill balloons with nitrous and pass them around, which forever changed my attitude about going to the dentist.

We arrived at the lab with Lanier to inventory the heads. They were kept in tall plastic buckets, most of which held two heads, sawed in half lengthwise and floating in formaldehyde. Mimi Lacarno's dad occasionally acquired a sheep's head that he would prepare for roasting by running it through a band saw from snout to spine and these cadavers displayed a similar cross section. But these had been human beings, generous souls who donated their parts to science, and even though the brain had been removed we all felt an immediate kinship. Not something you see every day.

Nor smell. We cracked open one bucket after another and poked around the murky stew with long tongs, trying to confirm just how many we had on hand. Lanier was the first to gag. I quickly followed, while we were perched on lab stools, bent over the buckets. An attendant pulled us away.

"Whoa, hey, don't puke on specimens! That's a real problem," he said.

We took a breather in an adjacent room. Lanier was more angry than sick.

"Dammit, you boys finish. I ain't doin' this shit. This is your case." With that, he returned to the station. Jack and I finished the inventory and counted eight complete missing heads.

We learned that each head would fetch five hundred to a thousand dollars on the black market. But the labs were always locked and we saw no sign of a break-in. After a dozen interviews and phone calls, we narrowed down our suspect list. One pathologist had left for Florida two days earlier, roughly the same time the heads may have disappeared. He would be on sabbatical, away six months without leaving a forwarding address with the university. Someone was picking up his mail but the school was leaning hard on us, holding witch-hunts within the department, while doing everything possible to keep a lid on the story. We didn't have all day to stake out a mailbox.

We took our evidence to Lanier, who learned that transporting cadavers across state lines is a felony. We dug up the make, model, and registration of the pathologist's car and Lanier alerted highway patrols along Interstate 95. Within six hours, the Georgia state police nabbed the doctor with the heads in his trunk.

He was not innocent; he had indeed sneaked the specimens away. A quick review of his sabbatical proposal showed that having cadavers to study would enhance his research. As for interstate transport, he was ignorant and cleared of any wrong-doing. Campus officials couldn't allow a reprimand without embarrassing the university.

By the time we finished the independent study, we concluded that there appeared to be an endless supply of greedy shakedown artists willing to prey on the poor. And we saw too many thieves, rapists, and gun-toting extortionists walk free. At the time, the courts were rabidly pursuing drug dealers and everything else was political penny-ante.

The project proved to me that I could exhaust my seemingly boundless curiosity by working as an investigator, because every lead teased me, every scrap of evidence promised a breakthrough and triggered a new creative strategy. But it also made me deeply cynical about the justice system. Jack and I struggled to write the final report, and I finished the year broke, disheartened, and with no idea of how to proceed. My summer job at the law firm waited for me, but it didn't pay much and I needed to make some real money—steelworkers' wages. So I repeated my May ritual of walking into the personnel offices at the mills, up to the tiny windows where women slipped application forms under the glass. It had a way of making me feel low, like a true supplicant, someone whose human contact was limited to a gap in a window, for whom an open door might be far too promising.

One morning, I sat down at my desk at the law firm, opened my briefcase, and mustered enough courage to peek at the statement the college loan agency had sent days earlier. I had a sense of how much I owed and could only bear to glance at the total. The figure darkened the entire room. More than my parents' mortgage. I bent over my desk to look down the hall at my boss cradling his bald forehead, proofreading stultifying documents, and my deflation might have been audible, as if the secretary would later find only a permanent-press wardrobe draped across the blotter.

She did poke her head in. "Hi, your mother's on line one."

"Hi, Sweetie," said Betty. "I thought you might want to know that Armco called."

"Oh, yeah?"

"They want you to call them back." She gave me the number. "Rudy said they were hiring. Are you going take a job there?"

With my free hand, I immediately began filling my briefcase with the few personal items on my desk. In that moment, the trappings of working in a law firm didn't matter. I was fulfilling a destiny. And how better to know Ambridge than to become a steelworker?

20

Of Heroes and Helpers

Twenty-six men and two women sat on a low bench facing canvas banners of Armco Steel and the United Steelworkers of America. When the personnel officer strode in, clipboard in hand, wearing a white short-sleeved shirt and a crew cut, we straightened up. He greeted us and passed out intake forms and told us he would see us after our physical.

Standing in line in my underwear reminded me of every story I'd heard about military induction. But in this situation, I prayed to pass. We submitted to the anticipated thumping, peering, and coughing on demand, donned blue shirts, work pants, and white socks, and padded back into the meeting room. The personnel guy handed out safety glasses and black boots with a steel shield that covered the laces from the toe to the top of the instep.

Surrounded by the smell of aftershave, floor wax, and the leather of my new boots, everyone and everything looked familiar. Behind my dreams of skiing the Alps, sailing the Caribbean, buttoning a Roman collar behind my neck, and arguing before a jury, stood the likelihood of this scene. It had always been possible. Now, finally, it was coming true.

"Some jobs'll last only through summer," the personnel officer said, "others'll continue on. Hard to say which." Consulting his clipboard, he told us to step forward when we heard our names.

"Kosis, Joe; Byoriak, Tom; Rossi, Bruno; Sokolowski, Chuck." He stopped, handed each of them a new white hard -hat and a badge with a four-digit number, sequenced in the order they were called. These numbers reflected seniority, so that Kosis had seniority over Byoriak, and on down. "Hot mill," he announced, and they headed out the back door.

He called names for the bar mill, the threading mill, the finishing mill, and the piercing mill, until only four of us remained, and all the white hardhats were gone, leaving four that had been painted orange. "Zelinski, Steve; Spolarich, Harry; Hertneky, Paul, and Sammartino, Emil; Mechanical Department, labor gang."

Labor gang sounded ominous, a lot like road gang or chain gang. Having my name called next to last made it sound worse. An old-timer with only three visible teeth escorted us to the Mechanical Department and told us to wait for the foreman who sat in a glass enclosure finishing paperwork, ignoring us. He seemed old enough to retire and scowled as he rose, as he met us without shaking our hands, and as he glanced at our files. He looked through the glass out toward the shop, craning his neck as if trying to find someone to blame, then walked away without a word. He was Frank Razano, known as "The Razor" behind his back.

I had only one man to pity more than myself: Emil, a pudgy family man who was thrilled to have a job. I mean thrilled, smiling the whole time, shifting his weight from one foot to the other, antsy to get to work. Without him, I would have been the lowest-ranking steelworker in a mill where 2,496 others could refuse an assignment before it came to us, and most jobs required two workers. The Mechanical Labor Gang was the last chance for morons, creeps, fighters, potheads, and drunks who had washed out of production jobs that required advanced skills like counting and cleanliness. They were the filthiest and most dangerous men in the mill and they all ranked above me and Emil.

That Sunday and every Sunday following, the two of us dropped into the bowels of the mill, dragging canisters of black goo, lubricating the mechanical beast overhead that heated and processed megatons of steel. On other days, we jackhammered, sometimes inside furnaces, drove spikes in the rail yard and shoveled mountains of metal shavings.

The mile-long plant stood on a bluff above the river. Its towering steel roof and black walls admitted light through tiny windows near the roofline. The operations on the floor were lit by hanging lights, preserving an overall gloom. For scale, picture a shopping mall minus the stores, with black walls and ceilings, its concrete floor a maze of machinery and catwalks.

From the rail yard, I could see Aliquippa's Jones & Laughlin plant, making steel downriver, where workers cast blooms from iron ore and coke, then finished them into cans, wires, and sheets. At Armco, we made seamless pipe from raw billets, but instead of buying the steel from the mill within sight, Armco bought them more cheaply from Korea and Japan.

Oil companies, drilling in new fields all over the world, bought Armco pipe as fast as we could make it. After two months, working seven days a week, sweating in greasy holes, breaking concrete and bending rails under the thumb of The Razor, I needed a change of scenery. Outside the mill, I found no time for anything but drinking and sleep. My parents saw it wearing on me. Milt knew the drone and the danger of mill work, which is why he found a way out. He never discouraged me from entering the mills because he knew I needed the money and he respected the way of life. But he also had deep doubts as to how long the industry might last.

Emil, or Emilio, as his mother called him, intended to make the mill his life. Every morning, we lined up shoulder-to-shoulder for roll-call and the day's assignments. One day, I noticed on the bulletin board a posting for a millwright's helper in the piercing mill. The posted jobs were temporary but carried a higher pay rate, so higher-ranking gang members usually snapped them up. No plum job had ever found its way down to me and Emil. Nonetheless, knowing Emil had kids and was always broke, I checked with him as the job worked its way down the line.

"Want this?' I whispered, looking straight ahead.

"No. Take it," he said, confirming that he had become content in his affection for a sixty-pound jackhammer. He slapped my back as roll-call broke up, and wished me luck. Helping a millwright, a skilled mechanic who kept the mill's machines running, promised a way to tolerate the desperate rut of jackhammering and shoveling, greasing the mill on Sundays. Any change of routine would do. At the same time, I worried why the job had drifted, unconsidered, down to me.

Through family connections, patrons, or protectors, my cohorts on the gang either knew the millwright or had been tipped off. I found out for myself that Rocky Marschuk, one of the oldest millwrights and one of the best, had no friends. His sullen nastiness repelled anyone who dared approach, and he went through helpers like a weasel in a warren of bunnies.

I waited for Rocky in the millwrights' shed, a ten-by-ten-foot cell with benches along two walls, adjacent to the piercing mill. When he walked in with his lunch bucket (literally, a pail with a lid), I hopped to my feet and introduced myself. He ignored my offered hand, only jerking his chin upward a quarter inch and glancing at me through the crossways buttonholes he had for eyes. He turned away and pulled a Dutch oven from a shelf, dropped it onto a hot plate, reached into his bucket and extracted a can of sauerkraut, cranked it open, and shook it into the pot. Then he threw in a loop of kielbasa, covered the pot and flipped on the burner. His routine.

"Ever done this job?" he asked while untying a bundle of shop rags, stuffing one into his back pocket. I told him no, and he shook his head and looked out the door at the racket of the mill. Then he walked out, scratching his stubble and mumbling "'ets go."

He issued a silent order by pointing to a grease canister like the ones I used on Sundays, and then strode ahead of me, silently touching the fittings—nipples on the mill's machinery that accepted grease. Their shiny brass stood out against the black motors and massive armatures. To service some fittings, we had to descend into a pit designed to catch errant pipes that were twenty feet long and glowing orange at two thousand degrees. That part of the routine scared the hell out of me. I watched and deduced that the trick was to quickly grease those machines before the pipes began to roll.

When we finished our tour of Rocky's section of the mill, he led me back to the shed where he examined a clipboard on the wall. I stepped out of the doorway as he noticed a man wearing a blue hard-hat—a production foreman—and intercepted him. Jabbing the clipboard with his finger, Rocky barked in the foreman's ear, who nodded. All I could hear was the roar of the mill.

Behind me, ten-foot-long bars traveled slowly around a donut-shaped furnace that heated them until they glowed like bright orange glass. At the end of their go-round, they fell into a slot of rollers that squeezed and stretched them as they passed through. Waiting for these nearly molten bars were the men who operated the piercing mill. One of them worked levers and pedals in a glass booth inside an A-framed structure that towered over the rollers. He controlled the propulsion of a long ramrod at the base of the machine that reared back, waiting for a soft bar to approach. Straddling the ramrod was a true roughneck, who used long tongs to fit the end of the piercing rod with a bullet-shaped bit. Once he placed the bit, the rod began spinning furiously under a torrent of cold water, then vaulted forward, ramming directly into the end of the oncoming orange bar. It reared back and rammed again and again, boring deeper each time, flakes of hot steel flying as the bar, clamped by rollers, picked up the spinning motion and finally gave way, and the piercing rod punched through, and then quickly backed out through a cloud of steam. The tortured new pipe rolled down the mill for finishing and cooling.

Howling machinery and high-speed collisions made a racket that would have drowned out a submachine gun. Rocky wore no ear protection and appeared to deliver his message clearly before turning away from the worried foreman. Calmer now, Rocky stepped back into the shed, hung his orange hardhat on a spike above the hotplate, folded a couple of shop rags into a pad for his head and stretched out on the bench along the wall. The aroma of kielbasa and sauerkraut had crowded out the smell of grease and smoking steel. With closed eyes he said, "Hit the fittings at two and four-thirty. Follow me when it blows five." Seconds later he was snoring.

I had to leave the shed to find an older production worker and ask him what Rocky meant. The production men and women wore white hard-hats. Millwrights and grunts like me in the labor gang wore orange, so we could be easily spotted deep within the mill's darkest holes and shadows.

"Oh, you're Rocky's helper? You poor bastard. Listen, do not fuck with him." The production worker bowed, shook his head, and spat, smearing the tobacco juice with his left boot.

"What he means is, when a piece of machinery breaks, we shut down the mill and call the millwright, givin' the whistle five shots." He reached up and touched a loop of steel cable attached to a steam whistle. "Time is money, and he'll be on the move. You better fuckin' be behind him."

"Does he just sleep until then?"

"Pretty much. Good luck," he said, walking away.

Everybody walked away from me. Nobody wanted to look at me or stand near me, as if I didn't have long to live, or at any moment, they might catch a piece of shrapnel. Back in the shed, I sat on the bench along the wall perpendicular to Rocky, leaned back against the cinder blocks, and stretched out my legs, crossing one heavy steel-toed boot on top of the other, then rested my hard-hat on my lap and closed my eyes.

Downtime punctuated every job in the mill. Lulls and waits and periods of boredom made the days longer. On a shoveling detail, for instance, I might fill a "bucket"—a dumpster-size box—with shavings, yank the rope of an air horn, calling the overhead crane, then wait and wait for it to come by and bring me another, taking the full one away. Millwrights, though, waited to be called and the best way to bide the time was sleeping. Arcane rules prohibited card-playing and reading. Something about the rules seemed reasonable; you wouldn't want to get too absorbed in a game or a novel.

Regardless of exhaustion, sleeping in a steel mill takes some getting used to. I stuffed my ears with soundproof fiber that looked like cotton. Wearing it was a sign of a short-timer, scared to lose his hearing and willing to risk ridicule. It made naps possible and I could hear enough. So, on this and one or two other matters, I took a hard posture inside the mill, like a convict, trying to protect myself. The attitude worked—

against hazing anyway. Other rookies suffered more abuse, adding to the cruel mystique of the labor gang. In the showers, greenhorns careless enough to bend over could be playfully violated with a bar of soap. As it turned out, nobody messed with me or Emil because they couldn't afford to lose the two guys at the end of the line. Without us around, someone else would have to take our jobs.

Half-deaf to the mill and Rocky's snoring, I drifted off. Every time a whistle blew, I snapped awake and instinctively reached for my hard hat. Then I'd see Rocky sleeping and I'd wait for the whistle again—only two bursts, or four. My movement woke him once. "Settle down," he said.

The next time I woke, Rocky was kicking the soles of my boots. I followed him out, counting five on the whistle. After twenty-five years as a millwright, answering the call of five, Rocky's subconscious had learned the drill. One of his neighbors told me that when Rocky slept on his porch across the river from J&L in Aliquippa, he woke up cussing when one of the mill's whistles blew five. Every time I slept through the call, he gave me hell, as if I should adjust, too. "And get the goddamn cotton out of your ears."

I stopped trying to sleep and stayed out of the shed, happy to grease my fittings on schedule and watch the mill in operation. At least once a shift, I noticed how a newly pierced pipe protested against the rollers and flared at the end, making it wobble down an incline toward the edge where I stood. One in a row of several armatures that rose up like forearms caught it, though, and sent it to another set of rollers, forcing it to comply, which I found comforting, especially because I had to stand in a pit at the bottom of that incline to grease the armatures.

Over two weeks, Rocky and I got by on fewer than ten

words a day. I was happy for the break from the jackhammer and railroad maul, the insipid shovel. Rocky treated me as dismissively as he treated everyone. I found peace in it.

We were passing the pit on the way back to the shed one night when Rocky noticed a leak in one of the hoses connected to the piercing mill while it ran at full tilt, maximum production, no time for shutting down the operation. I had fixed dozens of those hoses with him, meaning he had fixed, oh, sixty thousand. Amid the hellacious racket, he fished a clamp out of his pocket, a screwdriver and channel locks from his belt, and hopped into the pit. The operation was routine, a reflex. I crouched on the wall of the pit, ready to jump in behind him but he didn't want to be crowded, so he pushed me away with the back of his hand.

When I looked up, I saw one of the curled pipes flop out of the piercer. It jumped the first set of armatures, but I'd seen that before. The interruption in timing caused the second set of armatures to miss the pipe entirely and allowed it to pick up speed. Guys may have been shouting at this point; I don't know, my eardrums were protected.

By the time I screamed, Rocky was already watching the glowing two thousand-degree, one-ton pipe rumbling toward him, confident that the final set of armatures would catch it, never considering otherwise. Its flared tip canted the entire pipe into the air and sent it slamming down, dashing hot flakes through the sloping metal grate. The final set of iron arms reached up, corralling one end but slinging the other, and the pipe hopped over the armatures like a tailback at the goal line.

Rocky dropped his tools and spun, clutching the wall of the pit. I reached down, grabbed the shoulders of his shirt and fell backwards, taking him on top of me. The pipe crashed below us. He jumped to his feet, offered me his hand and yanked me up, then turned to look at the sizzling pipe, lying in the pit. "Yeah," he said. He squeezed my arm and shook his head. I trembled from heels to hard-hat.

The shift ended and word got around the locker room that Rocky had nearly been cut in half. Guys asked me questions, but I was still shaking and tried to say it was nothing. The men and women in mill prayed against all surprises, especially injury and death. Suddenly becoming a hero sounded stupid; I reeled between relief and residual terror. Adrenaline wouldn't let go. Over and over, I kept seeing that pipe drop past Rocky's feet. The guys rubbed my head and slapped my back, joking that maybe I should have let him die, that even in death, he'd probably wake up at the sound of five.

But Rocky knew the truth, and so did I. He thrust himself over that wall like a gymnast over a vault. I felt his raw strength. And because I felt his power, I knew he had saved himself. That's why it was okay that he hadn't thanked me. I hadn't even screamed in time.

Among my fellow workers, talk held little purchase. Every time I tried to explain that I did nothing, they told me to cut it out. "Nobody's gonna hate you for lettin' him live…except his wife," one guy said, and everybody laughed on the way to the showers. That morning, I had nothing to say, a rarity.

Rocky, the cruel and selfish antithesis of how I saw myself, robbed me of a chance to save him. He didn't need a hero. All these years I had been following a thread through a labyrinth, looking for every chance to slay a monster, and here I stood with only a child's fantasy lying at my feet. Feeling Rocky's wiry frame land on top of me had knocked the wind out of me, and cut a part of me loose. I had been set free from saving others. I could have been in that pit myself.

I drove home in my pale green Fiat, a comical hatchback I

had bought for $650 earlier in the summer, and went to bed.
When I awoke at three in the afternoon, I dressed for work.
I could still think of nothing to say, apart from telling my
mother that I was heading for the river until my shift started
at eleven o'clock. She asked me what was wrong. I said I was
tired. On impulse, she packed me three meatloaf sandwiches.

At the river, I found an old utility pole that had eddied out.
I sat on it and stared for a while, skipped a few stones, lay back
and watched the clouds. Boredom settled in, then a trance,
aided by the *thlip-thlip* of the water on the gravelly beach. I
rolled up my jeans and dragged the log closer to the water,
letting the tiny waves tickle my feet.

Christ on the cross, there he was, burnt into my
consciousness by kneeling through years of masses, the
ultimate hero, undeniably triggering the savior fantasies I had
created as a child. I wanted a happy ending, a rescue, but in
my boyish dreams I failed to come to terms with the hero's
essence—a readiness to step forward and die. I wasn't up for
that quest. More than anything, I wanted to live.

If I could no longer see myself as a hero, what new role
could I imagine? I let the question hang. I had nothing. All
my visions of the future suddenly lost their color and slipped
into a sepia of overuse and obsolescence. I grieved for them. I
stared across the river, until the silhouette of the power plant
crept over me, its smokestacks piercing the twilight, pressing
their outline into my skin like a crude tattoo, marking me as
a pipe-dreaming millworker. My lofty aspirations were unreal.
The smell of oil and sulfur, the taste of meatloaf and ketchup,
the dying light of another day—that was real.

Two centuries earlier, I might have been sitting on a birch
or pine log instead of a pole splintered by rung-holes and
stained with creosote. Industry had supplanted nature here,

just the way my own narrow ambitions crowded out the love that came my way from family, friends, and all those sweet women who let me hold their hands. And yet, in spite of the mills and slag piles, the lost settlements and forgotten history, the river flowed as ever, and when the stars came out, they held their place in the current.

By the time I passed through Armco's gates again, I felt numb, calm, and vaguely privileged to return. Rich Detz, a craneman and a friend from junior high, spotted me and dropped the iron hook of his crane behind me as I walked to the locker room. He sped up, chasing me. I picked up the pace as the hook closed in on my back. We had played this game before; I ducked and it whooshed over my head. I flipped him the bird and heard him laughing as he rumbled down the roofline of the mill.

Seated in front of my locker, I bent over to tie my boots and, to this day, I can still feel my cheek pressed against the cool grease caked on my pants from the night before. My fingers began to shake. I struggled with the laces and felt the hand of the foreman on my back. "Line up for a job tonight. Rocky wants a new helper." My head sank to my shins. I could go back to the comforts of a shovel or jackhammer.

Emil overheard the foreman. Now he would become the millwright's helper. I sat up, taking a deep breath of the solvents embedded in my uniform and the gooey Go-Jo we used to wash our hands. I had never imagined that stirrings of a new future would appear for me within the walls of a steel mill.

21

Untethered

Near the end of my summer as a steelworker, Armco offered me a permanent job. I had dismissed law school, and finishing a degree in English seemed pointless. I didn't want to be an English teacher and, in the wake of Woodward and Bernstein, the shoving matches for lowly journalism jobs made even the college newspaper a cutthroat enterprise. Deep in debt and without prospects, fat union paychecks felt like mining gold. But the labor gang? For an indefinite stretch? Sounded exactly like prison.

I set aside practical considerations like money and career prospects, dutifully registered for my senior year at Pitt, and gave notice at Armco. I'd been working sixty hours a week in a factory since May. I needed time off, a long draught of salt air, and the smiles of a woman who soothed me.

Coaxing the Fiat toward Massachusetts, I stayed awake by imagining the smell of Liz's hair, the pressure of her lips, the addictive quality of her laugh. The day after I arrived we set out to walk the six-mile strand of Duxbury Beach. The clouds laid a mottled roof over our heads, sending home the less hearty beachgoers and giving us long stretches of silence. We rolled our jeans up to our knees, tied our sneakers together, and walked into the onshore breeze. I told her I felt lost and rudderless, without destination.

She slipped her arm around my waist and said, "You're on your way."

"But where?"

"Right now, to that lighthouse," she said, pointing ahead.

"Carry me," she commanded, and hopped on my back. I held her knees against my ribs and trudged on. She pulled at my ears and asked if I wanted to drop her.

"No, I like this."

Into the top of my head she suggested, "Maybe you only need to be helpful."

"That's easy."

"And for you, it's natural," she added in a way I would remember.

She liked the word "natural" and threw it around a lot, because she thought nature needed more attention—our nature and the nature around us.

A few days later we had a fight outside McDonald's; Tom and Carol's kids wanted Happy Meals. The parking lot alone set her off, and the smell of searing flesh sent her over the edge. Her vehemence surprised me so much that I had trouble taking her seriously at first, but she grew angrier by the minute. I argued that it was easier to please the kids than make a political statement. Her reaction, though, was visceral, not intellectual. She stayed in the car while I convinced the kids to make a meal of French fries, a smell I hoped their aunt could tolerate. I wondered how many vegetarians ditched their boyfriends over disputed cheeseburgers.

Two days before returning to Pitt, I secured a nighttime job cooking and bartending in Mad Anthony's, the best restaurant in Ambridge. Having lost enthusiasm for my studies, I went through the motions, going to classes during the day and commuting back to my hometown—in the opposite direction of good sense several nights a week. Afterwards, I dowsed adrenaline in after-hours joints with other bartenders, waiters, and cooks. Not exactly a wholesome lifestyle.

One afternoon in late fall, I dashed to Ohio to visit Liz, and, from the moment we reunited, we acknowledged the widening gap between us. We tried to forget the McDonald's dustup, but we couldn't ignore that she had acquired a taste for essences and I a taste for poison. Her ethics stiffened when I couldn't resist giggling at spelt and millet; the words alone tickled me. More and more, she saw how she could make a complete life in Athens—growing her own food, making her own clothes, living off the power grid. I couldn't see myself as part of that life, even though I loved that she invited me into it.

Late one night in her dorm room, she put on a beautiful, gauzy nightgown that made me gasp, but instead of making love, we lay awake searching the ceiling for the words that described what we wanted most in life. I wanted to travel, to sail, to live in a culture I would have to decode. I wanted to improvise, follow ideas, live by my wits, and make money, enough to erase the worries I had known all my life. She wanted to have children and teach, nourish those around her, turn away from the material world and live off the land. What's more, she told me that she had been able to imagine that life more clearly because she had met a man who had been living that way in Montana, a wise, determined man who was several years older. She wasn't dumping me for him, but I could tell that she had begun to see a way to live the life she wanted.

We fell asleep holding each other, knowing it would be our last night together. The following morning, at peace with our decision, we set a tender tone for a friendship that would last for decades. As I drove home to Pittsburgh, though, sadness swept over me in the midst of a sleet storm following me from the west. Lost in a sense that important attachments were snapping their tethers and flying away, I hadn't noticed my car's tiny engine rattling furiously, until, with one resounding rap, it died and left me coasting onto the shoulder beneath an overpass. The Fiat snubbed me, as if offended that I had given up on *la bella Italiana*. I gathered my bags and hitchhiked into the city.

Another vision of the future—living by the sea with Liz where she taught in a local school and I came home after winning class action suits for single mothers and we'd catch the sunset from a modest sailboat—that I played out as I lay my head on my pillow every night, had been scattered in the wind. I fell asleep with books on my chest, and used Montaigne to guide me, responding to situations as they arose. The emptiness allowed me to focus. I paid attention in class, at work I embraced the stories of barflies, and I spent my free time with my father and friends who helped me replace the engine in the Fiat.

For thrills, I secretly spent nights with a waitress who was widely known for her skills as a tip magnet, a brilliant and attentive server who slipped her stunning physique into a dirndl. Think brunette St. Pauli Girl. Every man and more than a few women hit on Ricki and she responded by threading her hips around the tables, a tray of pitchers and steins held aloft, presenting it with a flourish and a dip that showed her muscular arms, her powerful legs, and carefully displayed cleavage.

She flirted with customers but always went home alone. Dogged regulars bought her expensive gifts. She said they shouldn't, but they did. She kissed their cheeks, stamping lipstick on their skin. She treated lecherousness as harmless, because she was in command. She set the boundaries. When pressed for details of her personal life Ricki described her boyfriend, a Marine, Military Police at that, she met while visiting North Carolina. Stationed in Germany, he came home irregularly and they loved each other desperately.

When I fell into the weeds behind the bar and in the kitchen she backed me up. She was five years older than me and her brio, as well as her non-hippie, old-school sexuality, scared me. I made her laugh, not just the compliant laugh she used with customers, but a laugh that burst out of her, made her swat me with a towel and bite her fist.

After we closed on a rollicking Saturday night, Ricki's car refused to start. I offered her a ride home and she invited me in—to the private quarters nobody I knew had ever seen. Unlike college girls, she owned lingerie, lots of lingerie. We told no one. Our assignations were covert. I often pictured the Marine walking in on us and killing me. But she was worth the terror and, in time, I learned that he was only a story, a protective fib.

To start a bartending shift at four o'clock, I finished my last class, ran to my apartment, grabbed my uniform, and dressed while driving to Mad Anthony's. My parents lived ten minutes from the restaurant and I could have kept uniforms there, where Betty would have been happy to launder them. But going there would have meant visiting and telling them more about my daily life of classes, working, fucking, drinking, classes, homework, drinking, fucking, working, and changing my pants while driving sixty in a forty zone through a gauntlet of traffic lights. I doubted they wanted to hear that.

When I tried to crystallize the future, I saw myself as one of millions of baby boomers with English Literature degrees. *TIME* magazine ran a feature about Harvard grads with degrees in English and philosophy who were driving cabs and waiting tables. I was already bartending and cooking—jobs I liked that promised little.

Early in that year, my grandfather wrapped up another day of working in the garden, drinking coffee, sneaking smokes, and watching television with my grandmother. The following morning, he failed to wake up. My grandmother took it as anyone reasonably happily married for fifty-three years might. But soon after Christmas (my grandfather's birthday), she suffered a kidney disease that landed her in the hospital in Pittsburgh, where she would die within a few weeks. Her hospital stay allowed me to take a break from the madness of my days, and sit with her during long dialysis treatments. I visited her once or twice a week. She couldn't talk much, so I read to her while she dozed. One night, I told her about wanting to someday live elsewhere, but I didn't know where and couldn't see how that might happen. She rolled her head to look at me, reached up with a hand taped to several tubes, and grabbed my scruffy beard. "You have the luck," she said, barely nodding and smiling, then continued, "Now give me some." She grabbed my hand and squeezed it harder than she ever had, for the last time.

22

Dodging a Bullet

One evening in March of my senior year, one steady customer I only knew as Teresa asked me what I planned to do after college. I admitted that I had no idea. She always wore navy blue or charcoal grey suits with crisp white blouses and we'd gotten to know each other after a hundred or so happy hours.

"When will you be finished?"

"The term's over in May, but I'll probably have to take another course or two to graduate." I'd gotten behind, wasn't studying, and knew I was about to boot at least one class.

She looked down into her Scotch and soda then right at me. "I could pay you a good salary, but I'd need you to start right away," and she gave me a look that showed regret. "I know you could do it. You'd be great at it."

She managed a trucking company, Wyner Commodity Lines, which specialized in moving steel, machinery, and refrigerated goods, and she needed someone to write forceful letters, deal with insurance companies and safety regulators, inspect trailers, and create press releases and ads. I liked the variety. And the salary she offered came close to what my roommate, who was about to get his degree in electrical engineering, had been offered by General Electric. I couldn't believe it.

Only decades later would I learn how disappointed my parents were at my decision to quit college—within sight of finishing. They kept it to themselves. Knowing that I had worked and paid my own way as far as I went, through meager times when they often worried for my health and safety, they accepted my decision. As always, they offered all they could give—love and emotional support. They had already convinced themselves that, as a good bullshitter, I'd ultimately be all right.

After meeting with the trucking company's personnel officer over Dewar's and soda days earlier to confirm that I had actually landed a job, I followed him into the owner's office across the hall. Jimmy O'Leary was on the phone and pointed across his desk to a beat-up leather chair. The fifty-ish redhead, a tall, rangy beast straight out of a Celtic battle scene, leaned on his elbows and laughed into the phone before saying, "Oh Christ! He's the one who shit the bed. Tell him to pay up or shut up." And he smiled at me while the caller laughed and said goodbye.

He dropped the phone on the cradle and lunged over his desk to shake my hand before I could rise to meet it. "So, I thought you were in college. What happened?" he asked as he picked up a Pall Mall that had been idling in an ashtray, took a drag and squinted through the smoke it left behind.

"I need a better job than bartending, sir," I said, surprised at his abruptness, "and I figure I can finish school anytime."

"What do your parents say about that? And don't fuckin' call me 'sir.'" He lay back in his vinyl chair and threw one leg up onto the credenza while adjusting his balls. At six foot six, and wiry, O'Leary looked like he could beat me to death, dice me into untraceable bits, and toss me in the river, just for calling him "sir."

"They understand. And I've been paying my own way."

"Teresa says you're a decent bartender. That you can handle drunks." Now there's a recommendation, I thought, considering all her friends are drunks, and I'm thinking the same about Jimmy.

"She's nice. I just try to stay calm. Treat everybody with respect," I said.

"Makes sense. You're gonna have to do the same around here. These drivers own their own rigs and they gotta be shrewd or they're out of business. Don't let 'em get over on you." He slipped another cigarette out of the pack and lit it. "They're gonna hide shit from you and lie to you. Keep an eye on 'em and talk to me or Teresa if somethin' doesn't add up. If you don't, they'll hand you your ass on a plate and say 'bon-fuckin' appetit," he said as he parked the smoke in his mouth and smashed his fist into his palm.

"I'll stay on top of it, sir," Damn! I couldn't believe I called him that. I got ready to duck.

"Don't let anybody scare you, kid. Most of these miserable bastards are reliable, so we try to keep 'em happy. Everybody should be happy workin' here. We got a saying, I think your buddy Teresa made it up: 'Get happy or get the fuck out!'" he said, laughing and coughing.

I didn't know whether to laugh or not, but I laughed anyway as the green-eyed tarantulan man pulled his white patent leather shoes to the floor and stood up. He shook my hand with a massive claw covered with scaly freckled skin and patches of red hair, all ten primary knuckles jutting out like walnuts around his long, tobacco-stained fingers.

I found an attic apartment in a two-story house alongside the Ohio River in Sewickley. The space had high dormers to the south, east, and west, where the light played and framed a view of the river. I could hear trains passing only a block away.

At an auction house nearby, I bought queen size mattresses, a comfortable sofa, and a desk for one of the alcoves. At last, I could live alone, which reminded me of the excitement I felt when I settled into my room at the Harrisburg Y.

When the frame of my little Fiat rusted and cracked beneath me in the middle of Ambridge, I felt the front tires rubbing madly against the wheel wells and wrestled it onto a side-street, up over the curb, and abandoned it next to a twisted chain-link fence behind a factory. The following day, I asked Milt to take me to a car dealer. I knew exactly what I wanted, and, amazed at its low price and gas mileage, my dad agreed with my choice.

My steady job allow me to buy a new, bright yellow Honda Civic—tiny, flashy, reliable, and, like the Fiat, comical. But the "Buy American" crowd didn't find it funny at all. As hard as it is to believe today, Japanese cars rarely appeared on American roads in the 1970s, almost never in the industrial heartland. My Civic was hard to miss. Twice, in the first week, passengers leaned out their windows and spit on it. Yes, two "patriots" spit on my car.

When I parked it in my parents' driveway, neighbors converged on it, asking me to open the hood so they could see the rubber band and chiding me for "helping the Japs." My boss told me to park it behind a shed while I was at work. I didn't care. It sipped gas and was cute.

After I learned the basics of my job, inspecting trailers, processing insurance claims, and working with background investigators to vet new owner-operators, I found it easy. Soon bored, I begged for more responsibility. At once, I became one of those over-eager young employees who makes the career clerks look bad. To keep me from pissing anyone off and to help the most beleaguered man in the building, Central

Dispatcher Ralph Jones, I was promoted to be his assistant. The job had me juggling ten phone lines and coordinating loads of steel at mills and freight yards from Sault Ste. Marie to Baltimore. It appealed to my affection for geography and my travel fantasies, while Jonesy, as Ralph was known, patiently taught me the ropes.

Without the burden of classes and homework, I read what I wanted, everything I wanted, stacks of Louis L'Amour that my grandfather had passed on to me. His stories took me out west, and Graham Greene took me elsewhere. Sewickley had a great library and I raided its shelves. Montaigne stayed on my nightstand. With a guitar, I insulted the ballads of Jim Croce and Gordon Lightfoot. I sent the vibes of Milt Jackson out to the river, staring at it most evenings until it was too late to see friends. No roommates. No siblings. Finally, I had enough money to pay my bills and make a dent in my student loans.

Three of my closest friends from high school were nearby and we saw each other on weekends. I tried to be a good brother and son, attending nearly every family gathering. They all made me feel secure and part of a clan. I began to see that, as a young man who had never been a victim of abuse or anything crueler than a little scarcity and dangerous work, had been spared fear, violence, and rotten luck, had known happiness and peace, I could keep on dreaming. I could stay light on my feet. I would always find work and a wonderful woman would come along when I was ready for her.

Had she already come along, and, in the frenzy in which I'd gone through college, had I missed an opportunity? That question began to haunt me as the monotony of daily office work introduced me, for the first time, to the effects of loneliness. Having failed to pursue a legal career or stay in school, I wanted desperately to succeed at my job, which demanded discipline and cast me into a predictable, hypnotic pattern that paralyzed my enthusiasm and made me feel like an office drone. The only time I felt alive was when I came home to a letter, sent *Par Avion* from Brazil.

After finishing grad school in Michigan, Mimi Lacarno took a six-month vacation in Brazil to visit girlfriends she had met while they were exchange students in Ambridge. Every letter and postcard she sent—from Rio, Recife, Brazilia, and Sao Paolo—fanned my travel fires and simultaneously set flame to a yearning I had never felt for her. Was it envy, or simply her absence? Was it the ordinariness of my new life, or was it the way she wrote to me: full of joy, discovery, openness, and confessing that she missed me? I tacked her letters to the wall in front of my desk, where I could look up and read them again and again.

Coming home after work, I noticed how the slant of the setting sun downriver signaled the end of summer. For the first time in three years, I had not traveled to the beach in New England and I missed Liz, the dunes, swimming in the sea. My job in Central Dispatch may have been hellish from early morning until 5:00 p.m. but it left my weekends free. One Friday, I shot home, grabbed a duffel bag, a cooler, a tent, books, my guitar, and jumped into the Civic. I knew where I had to go.

East would take me to the Jersey shore, at least six hours away, and even then, I'd be stuck in late summer traffic. Instead, I hopped onto the interstate and drove north in a straight line to the nearest watery edge of the nation—Presque Isle State Park on Lake Erie. As daylight faded, I found a campground with cabins for rent. The lake's reputation as a polluted reservoir worked in my favor; a cabin was cheap and available.

Sitting on the doorstep, my back against the screen door,

I drank tall-boys, gulped the fresh and fishy breezes as if I had just come up for air, and watched the moon rise over the vast lake. I dug out a Zane Grey novel that I'd lifted from my grandfather's stash and read under the light of a bare yellow bulb that almost kept the mosquitos away.

Solitude wrapped its arms around me as Liz would when we sat on the jetty, and I stared at the lake's sea-like horizon. As always, it raised the narcissistic question, what's out there for me? I didn't utter a word all weekend and the neighboring vacationers paid me no mind. I ate junk food and peaches, ran along the beach in the morning, swam, then started drinking beer and chewing tobacco (a legal buzz I learned to like while playing softball) and spitting in a paper cup. I've always had a five o'clock shadow well before three, and by Sunday I took on the air of certified hobo.

When I got home, I peeled all of Mimi's postcards and letters off the wall and read them again. Most of them described her day, her friends, and their adventures, but others told me that she missed me and wished I could be traveling with her. She revealed far more about herself, her reactions and responses to the nuanced challenges of travel and what they taught her, than she ever had in person. She signed them all "Love, Mimi."

When her final letter arrived a few days later, I noted when the Varig flight would be landing, and the timing of her connection to Pittsburgh. Without hesitation, I arranged to fly to La Guardia in advance of her arrival, and booked a ticket on her homeward connection. Impulse. I decided, after five years of equivocation and watching our relationship follow a beta wave of attachment and distance, I was eager to make a grand gesture, and prepared to look like a fool.

I kept the plan to myself. Nobody understood my relationship with Mimi. Not my friends or my family. Oh, she was sloe-eyed gorgeous, serene, kind-hearted, and she laughed easily, but all that just made everyone want to know more and she offered no access, rarely spoke and never about herself. She looked hot but she ran cool, seldom showing anger, excitement, or any strong emotion. I knew her reticence was natural, not some sort of passive aggressiveness. Like Liz, she played no psychological games, which I found all too common and tiresome among young women, and she took more interest in understanding others than in making herself understood. On the surface, she seemed mysterious at best and dull at worst. I knew her as well as anyone.

Her flight from Brazil was set to arrive early on Saturday morning. The only flight to La Guardia I could get landed at 10:30 on Friday night. As soon as I arrived, I took a cab to Kennedy. I got my first look at the Unisphere outside Shea Stadium, and I could barely contain my excitement. I found the massive departures board, with its clicking, flipchart letters and numerals, the names of cities from Ankara to Warsaw—an icon of the jet age, the Cold War, and international intrigue. Mimi's flight from Rio, still six hours away, had yet to appear on the board. Around midnight, after walking the entire length of the airport and shutting down a cocktail lounge, I was alone in front of the arrivals board. I spread out my jacket on the platform, lay my head on my knapsack and dozed, waking every time I heard the rapid *rat-a-tata-tata-tata-tata-tata* of new information, my heartbeat rising to match the rhythm.

Mimi's jaw dropped at the sight of me, standing there like a character out of a Neil Simon comedy, rumpled, unshaven, and holding some silly flower. Her look made it all worthwhile. She was also drained from thirteen hours of flying and seemed disoriented. In the cab to La Guardia, she kept turning to me and shaking her head. "I can't believe you did this!" she said again and again. I may have wished she was showering me with kisses, the way a Goldie Hawn might have gushed, but then I remembered, Mimi was more of a nuanced Natalie Wood. She seemed more worried by my effort to meet her and my willingness to sleep in the airport than happily impressed.

All the youthful designs and plans that had kept me from falling in love with her had dissipated, and I felt passion like never before. Forget about the traps of commitment. Forget about living elsewhere. I risked setting in motion a series of events that would keep me near home for life. Mimi liked Pittsburgh. Her aging parents would need her. She wanted a secure job as an occupational therapist and a regular paycheck, no further adventure necessary. Brazil had been enough.

Only two days after she had been strolling along the sand at Ipanema, the two of us picked through the underbrush on a hike along the banks of the Ohio River. She had to be reeling from the contrast.

I couldn't wait any longer to tell her what I'd been feeling, and expected she'd been waiting for it. We sat on a hummock where we could watch a half-dozen barges labor their way upstream. I told her how I waited for her letters and missed her every day. I apologized for my years of involvement with other women and the heartache I must have caused. Then I announced, for the first time in my life, that I was in love—with her.

She cried and took my hand. Hanging her head, her hair around her face, she said, "I'm sorry. I'm so sorry."

I had missed a few signs. Surprising her at LaGuardia failed to elicit the desired response. Shock, yes. Unbridled joy, no. I excused it as jet lag. Among the gifts she'd brought home—colorful weavings and handmade hats—she gave me a keychain she bought in the Rio airport. That should have tipped me off. I told her I loved her partly because I promised myself I would. Her change of heart surprised and crushed me, leaving me without a sense of what to do next.

She called me three days later. "You want to come over for dinner? I got my pictures back." Of course I did. I was heartbroken, but the attraction of seeing her, of eating with her family, hadn't ended. I wondered what was in those pictures that might give me a clue about her change of heart.

Many of Mimi's local girlfriends made the dinner more lively than usual and we passed the photos around the table while Mimi pointed out who was pictured. The snapshots showed the two Brazilian friends—both stunning women—who had been exchange students in Ambridge, their families, their friends, at home, on side trips, and lots of eye-popping bikini shots of Mimi and her traveling partners playing on the beaches at Recife and Ipanema. No men, for the most part. I would find no hint of a rival in Brazil.

Mimi returned to college, three hours away, in the fall. But she stayed in touch with me, writing notes and asking me to call her. When she came home, she wanted to see me, have me come to her parents' house, as if we could always be friends, and she was right. We made a habit of staying in touch over the ensuing decades and still make each other laugh, but it's all too easy to imagine what life might have been like with her—provincial, family-oriented, quiet to the point of puzzling. She spared me the suffering, and I soon felt like I had sidestepped a bullet that summer, and before it was over, I had dodged two.

23

Itching All Over

Firmly ensconced in my first career-like job out of college, with dreams placed on hold and loans to repay, I dove into work. To see it today, Central Dispatch at the trucking company would stand as one of those complex analog work settings that would be transformed overnight by the digital age. Jonesy and I occupied half of an office bisected by a waist-to-ceiling Plexiglas wall. We scooted on high, wheeled drafting stools, before a slanted surface, much like a drafting table, but running the length of the room and attached to the wall we faced. Lining that wall were vertical rows of metal time-card slots, dozens of them, mounted side-by-side and labeled at the top with the names of cities east of the Mississippi, north of Tennessee and the Carolinas, all the way to the tip of Nova Scotia—left to right, west to east, our geographic domain. Each of our contracted trucks, our owner-operators, was represented by a card.

Working two phones with multiple lines, we received and placed calls from dispatchers in each of the cities who served manufacturers of metals and machinery as well as foodstuffs. Our drivers mostly towed flatbed trailers for the manufactured goods and refrigerated trailers for the food, both lucrative because the more expensive or perishable the load, the higher the shipping rate. Jonesy and I fielded calls continuously from

7:00 a.m. until 5:00 p.m., trying to keep every truck loaded to capacity and every dispatcher satisfied with the timely pickup and delivery of every load.

All day long we punched blinking buttons, talking with hard-boiled, hopped-up, or hung-over drivers who screamed at us from truck-stop or roadside pay phones about the *lazy shit-eating ass-packers* who sloppily strapped a load of *motherfucking* scrap metal he picked up when we had promised him expensive hydraulic pumps. Dispatchers, like Roy—a compact Brando-type guy with Camels rolled in his shirtsleeve, sitting on the other side of the Plexiglas and covering Pittsburgh's industrial complex—passed along threats from shippers verbatim, in language that would offend a gangster. Roy was a former dump hauler (the true madmen of truck drivers, who pull long dump trucks for short distances at reckless speeds, usually with tarps rolled over the top), a family man and dirt-track race driver on Saturday nights. We kept 475 drivers with various mental illnesses rolling as fast as they could along 10,000 miles of highways. When snowstorms swept through the territory, all hell broke loose.

My boss, Jonesy, a seven-year veteran with a stake in the business, drove the operators like rented mules. Quick-witted, alert, and accurate, with natural warmth and ice-cold negotiation skills, he took no shit and multitasked better than any line cook I'd ever worked with or have seen since. He also weighed about 260, torched fifty smokes on a slow day, bit his nails to the quick and lay under a spigot of vodka every night. But he never came in late, never struck me with anything but his open hand, and treated me like a favorite little brother. In a way, he had to, since nobody else had lasted in the second chair for more than three weeks.

Jonesy arranged for me to get bonuses and, together, we

made lots of money. But he and big Jimmy and other guys in the office maintained habits that demanded larger sums. In addition to smoking, drinking, and infrequent prostitutes, Jonesy ran off to Vegas on weekends, calling me one Sunday night from the airport using the last dime in his possession. Young and resilient, I held my own with my workmates, but socially, their drunken belligerence and readiness to brawl unnerved me.

The intensity of my job distracted me, but at home I waited for letters or calls from Mimi that very seldom came. Otherwise, I sought the comfort of my friends, but after working with drivers all day who covered enormous distances and loved the road, I felt my home turf closing in around me. Making my rounds in Sewickley, Ambridge, and Pittsburgh, driving the same routes over hills, ridges, and rivers, seeing the same people, made me crave space and new vistas. In absence of real adventure, I holed up and dreamt through fiction, tearing through Hemingway's entire canon again, all the sailing and traipsing throughout Europe. I ran to the city on Saturdays to sit in front of Gauguin's Polynesians then tuck into one of my favorite jazz joints where I could float away. Every night, in order to fall asleep, I pictured myself on a Cape Cod beach or in a café in San Sebastián.

When the steelhaulers called a national strike in mid-June, I called Mimi's brother, Vinny, a talented folk singer who was often between gigs, and invited him to join me on a road trip. We packed the Civic with a tent, a cooler and a couple of guitars and headed for Cape Cod, where we camped on the beach for a few days until driving up the coast toward Boston.

Tom and Carol had recently sold their cottage and moved to a suburb nearer the city. With plenty of room for guests, they welcomed us to stay as long as we liked. The change of venue made it easier for me to be there without Liz, though I still missed her, and Carol told me she'd be visiting later, with her husband, a man they both very much liked. At one point in the visit, I took particular note that I had been sharing meals and sofas with Mimi's brother and Liz's sister. It all seemed somewhat incestuous.

Hanging out on Nantasket Beach one afternoon, the remarkably handsome Vinny attracted the attention of two local girls, bikini-clad knockouts, the type that usually looked straight through me. They smiled when they came near, fiddled with their gold neck chains, and said hi to Vinny.

"Hi," he said, as they slowed. "Nice day, huh?"

"You kiddin'?!" one said. "It's pissah, wicka pissah!"

"What?" we both asked.

"You know, wicka nice, wicka pissah!"

Still stumped, Vinny asked what they were talking about. Instantly, they saw us as exotic vagabonds who needed to be introduced to local culture. At the end of the afternoon with the girls, both of whom were hanging on Vinny, he said to me, "I see why you like it up here."

We stayed with Tom, Carol, and their three daughters as long as we could. Before leaving, I fantasized with them about moving to Boston. They encouraged me to come and invited me to crash with them until I got a place of my own. Vinny, a homebody from birth, a man who has now lived in his parents' house for his entire life, got a glimpse of how quickly circumstances could change.

The first day I returned to Central Dispatch, I noticed that my chair had been switched with Jonesy's, nearer the window. And I could now see and hear the adjacent highway through two big bullet holes in the pane.

"What happened?" I asked.

"Steelhaulers are still on strike. Last week some shithead thought we were loading scabs," Jonesy said.

"You weren't?"

"Fuck no! You kidding me? I stayed open to load boxes and reefers."

"Anybody get hurt?"

Jonesy shook his head. "It happened at night."

"So I'm by the window?"

"Yeah, you've been promoted."

After the strike ended, I tried to ignore the bullet holes. But struggling to fill trucks—as industry slowed and our busy swathe of the country began to rust—proved too hard. It wrung me out. We sent more drivers to Baltimore and Newark, where longshoremen loaded their flatbeds with containers full of imports.

One month later, I told my parents that Tom and Carol had offered me a bedroom in their house if I were to move to Boston. Milt and Betty weren't surprised. They wanted me to follow my instincts, confident that I would make a successful transition. In later years they admitted the sting of hearing my plans, but were happy I could stay with family.

Still uncertain, I consulted my two closest friends. Bob was finishing his senior year at Pitt and Rege had started an apprenticeship as a steamfitter. He had done a few turns in New Jersey, but Pittsburgh, Ambridge—western Pennsylvania—was home; it was all we knew. I worried about missing my family, mostly my siblings, but my friends could tell I was itching all over. They knew my family would always be there for me, and they assured me that my friends, those who were worthwhile, would be there too.

I thought Jimmy O'Leary, the bloody-knuckled president of the trucking company, would punch me in the face when I gave notice. True to his advice—that unhappy employees "get the fuck out"—he nearly congratulated me as we shook hands for the final time.

As a result of working for O'Leary, no boss would ever scare me again. I could fear losing a job, but Jimmy made me afraid of losing blood and teeth. I'd lived and worked with steelworkers, and yet, this milieu took rough language to Olympian heights. Jonesy taught me how to negotiate with truly mean and angry customers—shipping agents and hardened over-the-road truck drivers—by using aggressive assertion, cool threats, and giving way without surrendering. From those days forward, I give wide berth to tractor trailers and dump haulers on the road, knowing how exhausted and high they can be. The job that triggered my dropping out of college humbled me and showed me how much I would need to hustle and claw my way in the working world. Most of all, and oddly enough, it qualified me for my next job, and vaulted me into a life I hadn't dared imagine.

24

Like Ambridge with a "C"

I packed everything I owned into the Civic and hit the road. While driving, I thought about my grandparents, aunts, and uncles, all those immigrants eating and drinking around the table above me when I was a kid on Sunday afternoons, how they traveled to Rotterdam, across the ocean, then deep into the continent to find a place to sleep in a cousin's attic, and soon a job. Going the opposite direction, I was following suit, into arms of a kind cousin and his wife. After thirteen hours of driving, I caught a whiff of the Atlantic again and this time felt relieved that I could stay.

Apart from my cousins, I knew no one in Massachusetts. Any leads for a job would have to come from the newspaper. Now I could finally prove Betty's adage wrong: I could find work based on what I knew not who I knew. I studied the classifieds and pursued every lead, traipsing through Boston and Cambridge, trying to learn my way around.

One hot afternoon in August, I rode the subway to Central Square in Cambridge and walked toward Harvard Square, where a street hawker sold me a colorful tabloid, a weekly that carried stories about Love Canal, Lou Reed, and a dessert called tofutti. After walking a few blocks, I saw a new sign in front of a modern office building that read *The Real Paper*, the name of the tabloid under my arm.

The elevators opened to a floor plan typical of newspapers: business offices to one side with big windows and a nice view, and a dark, editorial slum on the opposite side. The receptionist, a beauty with long dreadlocks snaking around her headset smiled when I asked if I might talk with someone about a job there. Within moments, a spritely woman in a skirt and pumps, one of the few grownup types within sight, came out to meet me.

"What are you looking for?" she asked.

"I'm wide open," I blurted, handing her my resume.

She ushered me to her office where I talked about the trucking company, my move from Pittsburgh and what I had done at college. The questions went on and I began wondering if I might finally get a job on experience and enthusiasm alone, without strings and connections.

Her phone rang. She said, "Yeah, okay. I will." I could tell the responses were timed with a muffled voice I heard from another cubicle. After hanging up, she told me about selling advertising. It sounded dreadful. She also said that editorial jobs open occasionally and I could try writing one article at a time but the pay was lousy. She promised she would keep me in mind for selling ads. I would have done anything she asked—the office held a kind of youthful energy I hadn't seen anywhere and I could easily imagine how much fun it could be to work there. But as she shook my hand and offered a perfunctory promise to call me, I felt hope dwindling.

"Oh, and Dave Semple wants to see you."

"Who?" The name sounded familiar.

"Dave Semple. He said he knows you from Pitt."

He occupied the adjoining cubicle and I recognized him immediately as being a class ahead of me, though we hardly knew each other. A stiffly formal guy who had grown up in one of Pittsburgh's affluent suburbs, Dave had taken over as circulation director a year earlier. He shook my hand and asked me to wait in a seat next to Kita, his pretty assistant. The walls were covered with maps of the city, the state, and all of New England—my kind of décor. I smelled Dave's cigarette smoke and heard the whoop of a salesman making a sale as he dropped the phone on its cradle. An editor popped in to see if Kita was busy for lunch. *The Real Paper*—with its patron, David Rockefeller, in the corner office, was the pulse of the youth culture in Cambridge.

After a short interview, Dave offered me a job. My knowledge of trucking and transport systems helped. I would be charged with visiting newsstands and distributors, but the power of the Pittsburgh connection made all the difference. Once again, Betty was right.

Two weeks after I reported for work, a Friday night in September of 1978, after making sure the paper had gone to the printer, I crossed the street to The Plough and Stars for beers and hippie lasagna. The editors, artists, and ad sellers soon splintered off, leaving me alone with the cash from my first paycheck pulling me into Harvard Square.

Students returning from summer break filled the Square, chattering four abreast, oblivious to traffic and crosswalks. I had never seen such wild disregard for traffic or safety. Drivers jabbed their brakes and horns as they crept through clusters of bewildered freshmen and excited sophomores leaning in to hear each other's stories. Professors gazed at the pavement, murmuring a lecture or allowing madness to move their lips. They all strode at a brisk clip, sidestepping browsers at newsstands and head-bobbers squatting in alcoves and doorways where folk singers played for pocket change.

At the corner of Mass Av (they all said "av" never avenue)

and Boylston, I stopped to get my bearings. My nose followed the perfume of girls in boots and miniskirts, their Carol King-ish hair riding the breeze off the Charles River. The men were dressed in wrinkled linen and faded jeans. Some wore berets and pored over chessboards on streetside tables, their chins resting on their fists.

I had explored Harvard Square a few times that month, but as the students returned, I realized that I'd seen their ilk only in *Life* magazine's stories about American youth traveling abroad and ski bunnies of the eastern slopes. The Sixties and early Seventies had brought counterculture into this scene. Harvard students were portrayed on television and in film as precocious law students, apologists for Timothy Leary, sitters-in and protesters. In their midst, I was drawn to their sense of purpose, their enunciation, their understated layers of cotton and tweed and their quiet talk of horses and squash. One day they would be pulling the strings and working the levers that determined world events.

I had embarked on a new adventure, now eight weeks in Boston, and my job in the circulation department of the paper gave me a sense of permanence. I would move out of my cousin's house, rent an apartment, and find my footing among these people who had an entirely different bearing than I did.

When I looked down, I saw the wrongness in my shoes. They were two-tone, black and grey, something Sonny Corleone might wear. I fingered my gauzy shirt and thought I might be trying too hard. But these were the 1970s and who cared about clothes? I was the age of a graduate student, had big hair, and moved easily among strangers.

Near the center of the Square, I heard the blues rising out of the doorway to a basement music club named Jonathan Swift's. I sprung for the cover charge and descended into the squeal of slide guitar. After buying a beer, I found a place to stand behind a few rows of seats, closed my eyes and drifted along the swells of a saxophone solo. I separated the odors and then let them blend again: beery floorboards, summer bodies, hot amplifiers, cigarettes, marijuana breath, and Herbal Essence shampoo. The long hair of the girl standing next to me kept tickling my forearm and I didn't want to interrupt it, so I held my eyes closed and fell into the music.

Applause called me back to the room and I looked down to see the woman beside me clapping, tossing her hair to the side until she reached over her head with her other hand and pulled it behind her ear. Nice beaded earring, I thought. She smiled at me, then looked back to the stage, sipping from a plastic cup.

"I just love John Mayall," she said, turning her green eyes toward me.

She surprised me; I hadn't expected her to speak. And I knew nothing about Mayall. "Why?" is all I could squeeze out.

She said something like, "His blues find me."

I don't remember what I said, only that she asked, "Are you from around here?"—a question I took to mean that I didn't appear to be a student.

"No. You?"

She was from Evanston, Illinois, which, geography-freak that I was, I knew was outside Chicago. For some reason, though, I hadn't expected her to ask the same question, and a precise answer might crack the new persona I had been fashioning for myself.

"And you?" she asked.

"Oh, a little town, outside Pittsburgh."

"Which one? What's its name?"

"It doesn't matter."

"Yes it does," she shot back, a little perturbed.

"Ambridge"

She asked me to spell it, so I did.

"Oh, like Cambridge without the 'C'?"

I was struck by the similarity, which began and ended with that initial letter "C." Cambridge, originally Newtowne, renamed to match its aspirations—its eventual power and privilege, erudition and stateliness, all its history and money, presidents, preachers, and philosophers, its rowers pulling sculls down the Charles, sweating for sport. Ambridge, originally Economy, named for its landlord, The American Bridge Company—its steel, smoke, and football, corruption and soot, its displaced immigrants and fractured languages, thugs and brawlers, bookies and mobsters, bargeloads of ore and coal grunting up the Ohio, where nothing but carp and catfish could survive. Cambridge, a tangle of streets lined with bookstores and libraries, galleries and museums, coffee houses, theaters, dormitories, and think tanks. Ambridge, a simple grid of company houses, bars, churches, pizza joints, machine shops, Sons of Italy, Polish Falcons, factories, vegetable patches, alleyways, all-night diners, shrines to the Virgin, more bars.

The Mayall fan's comparison triggered this psychic excursion and when I snapped out of it, I looked all over the dark basement and tried to catch a whiff of her, but she was gone. She was interested enough to ask about me, to demand an answer. How could I let her slip away like that? Where had I gone? I was trying to immerse myself in this new place, to forget about Ambridge, and one simple mention sent me off into space. She probably thought I was stoned.

I had entered my imagined land of milk and honey. Like my grandparents, in that moment I put my old home behind me and looked ahead. In the decades that followed, mill towns dying along rivers became a cliché melded together as The Rust Belt. In the years to follow, I tried to shake the effects of growing up there: the hillbilly twinges within my diction, a millworker's class anxiety, a cynical edge to my natural optimism. I wanted to shed all that, but I also felt a son's attachment.

25

Rust: The Patina of Possibility

Between 1979 and 1986, Armco, American Bridge, A. M. Byers, National Electric, and several other factories closed, leaving dilapidated structures and mountains of scrap behind. Taken together, the abandoned, ruined real estate covered nearly four hundred acres. Aliquippa's mammoth Jones & Laughlin had become LTV Steel, shrunk, and closed, spreading joblessness throughout the valley.

Walking the length of Ambridge over the past couple of decades would take me from the gates of Armco to the school and church where I'd lost myself in heroic fantasies. Until very recently, I saw only signs of decline. Plywood covered more storefronts on Merchant Street, vandals tore away the bronze lampposts in front of the library, the streets crumbled with neglected potholes. For Sale and foreclosure signs sprang up like weeds as desperate residents abandoned their families for service jobs in the promising Sun Belt. Throughout the 1980s and '90s, as the owners of houses and apartment buildings moved south and lost their properties or their paying tenants, the buildings fell into disrepair. Landlords accepted government assistance that required them to take in unsavory tenants, addicts, prostitutes, pimps, and gangsters. The streets, especially those in the southern end of town around Divine Redeemer and my father's office at the bridge company, grew dangerous with crime. The already limping Catholic diocese of Pittsburgh closed several churches, including Divine Redeemer.

Several of the neighborhood bars closed. A few became hangouts for crack dealers and whores, but more hung on as cool, dark gathering spots for workers and harmless drunks.

My father, at only fifty-five years old, was forced to retire from American Bridge after thirty years of service. He joined one of the small drafting firms that cropped up throughout the valley, taking in work from all over the country, awarded to the lowest bidders. And the bidding was fierce. The combination of the steel industry's demise, a global oil crisis, and a national recession created a ripple effect that idled 153,000 workers in the Pittsburgh area alone. Within a five-hundred-mile radius, nearly a half million men and women lost their jobs.

Of all Rust Belt cities, Pittsburgh came down hardest and fastest, hitting rock bottom, allowing it to recover more quickly than Youngstown, for instance, which had one foot in the auto industry. In Ambridge, the blight has abated. Some of the factories found new uses as warehouses and were soon surrounded by tractor trailers, giant dumpsters, boxcars, and mountains of pallets. The A. M. Byers plant on the site of Legionville became such a terminal for a while, and the former Armco is a fully modern storage facility and light manufacturing center.

In the neighborhoods, I began to see new masonry and carpentry, tended gardens, and fresh coats of paint. A three-story company-built house held its own between identical houses ready for the wrecking ball. My aunt's ceramics shop, filled with mallards frozen in flight, Virgin Marys, leprechauns, and gabby hobbyists, defied economic odds. The Maple Restaurant, owned by the Pappas family since 1963, continued to serve heart-stopping portions, including a hot roast beef sandwich topped with French fries and gravy. The proud sign in the parking lot still reads, "Welcome to Hot Beef Country."

Students and faculty of The Trinity Episcopal School for Ministry brought fresh energy and optimism to town, counseling families, helping the poor, the sick, the dying, the mentally ill, and the lonely. Seminarians bought houses within the safer neighborhoods of Ambridge, sharing backyards and gardens with older Bridgers and young, struggling families. They began to look after children, mow lawns, and shovel sidewalks for those who otherwise shuffled to the pharmacy. They may have had an evangelical agenda, but they remain gentle and genuine compared to the economic and political hooligans that once ruled the streets.

Pittsburgh hung on. From 1970 to 1990, its population fell by more than 21 percent, and the exodus continued for another ten years. With its back against the wall, the city slowly reinvented itself, drawing on academic and health care institutions that serve the young and old. Its elderly population demanded innovative local health and rehab centers, and the medical infrastructure responded, providing a model for serving aging boomers. Their grandchildren needed education that would allow them to stay nearby and the city's public schools have become some of the best in the nation.

Overnight, in 2006 Pittsburgh went from having the oldest mayor in the country, at seventy-six, to the youngest mayor, at twenty-six, portending a youth movement in the city. Low housing costs, a burgeoning arts scene, and a variety of slowly recovering urban neighborhoods have attracted a young, creative class seeking fertile ground for new ideas.

Pittsburgh has shown remarkable adaptability that reminds me of one of the Rust Belt's most emblematic buildings—the former headquarters of U.S. Steel. Soon after the building was designed and commissioned in 1968, Milt brought home a brochure about it. At sixty-four stories, it would be the tallest building in the skyline. Its triangular shape and orientation echo the city's well-known triangle; but its skin is most telling—Cor-Ten Steel with a pre-oxidized surface, rusty from the outset, a deep brown patina that responds to weather conditions by healing itself. Favored by sculptors Robert Indiana and Richard Serra (a former steelworker), Cor-Ten presents a renewable aesthetic, an ongoing work in progress.

One evening while visiting home, I made plans for a reunion dinner with Mimi Lacarno. It had been four years since I'd moved to Boston, and I'd gotten married and moved to Atlanta. Mimi and I arranged to meet at Station Square in Pittsburgh, a converted railroad station on the banks of the Monongahela River. Near the entrance, I spotted a massive industrial relic that had been enshrined in the middle of the plaza, and it looked familiar. Its proportions and shape struck me—about thirty feet tall and formed like a giant beer barrel made of heavy iron, rusty but now shellacked for preservation. I recognized it, but the closer I got, the less I could believe my eyes—Bessemer converter #1 from the A. M. Byers plant in Ambridge, the heart of Vulcan's nightly show of sparks and molten iron I had watched from the back seat of my parents' Ford.

Mimi came up behind me and took my arm. "I know," she said. "Can you believe it?"

"No, I can't. It's like a shrine."

"To what, though?" she asked.

"A sacred place, I guess." We both laughed.

"Yeah, right," she said.

The monument set the tone for dinner, for the "what ifs"

that punctuate the past. During dinner she asked whether I would have married her back then if she had still been in love with me. I told her I didn't know. If she had leapt into my arms back then, I might have stayed in town, loading trucks and settling down. But the lure of travel and exploration was too strong and, if I had ignored it, the ground would have shifted under me. I suppose, by my declaration, I had indeed asked for her to come along. Instead, her goodbye had cut me loose.

26

Rescue Amid the Ruins

Regardless of how far I travel and how long I stay away, I will always be a Bridger. I knew it soon after leaving the Mayall fan in Jonathan Swift's, when I sat on the steps of Widener Library in Harvard Yard and, instead of dreaming about the future, I compared the scene to sitting on the steps in front of Laughlin Library, watching the steelworkers pass by. Particular aspects of the past can't be left behind.

If I had dreamt about my future, I would have been short of the mark. Right there between Harvard and Central Squares in Cambridge, in 1980, I met Robbie Palmer, a beautiful, brilliant introvert who was well out of my league. Struck by our deepest similarities and smitten with our many differences, we fell in love on our first date. The following morning I looked in the mirror and pictured myself twenty years older, still living with her. We married ten months later. Since that day, she has endured my curiosity by matching it with her own, embraced my wanderlust through a readiness to keep on moving for years until we found an ideal rural town in which to settle. A tireless reader and now a professor, she has kept me guessing and fascinated for decades. She shares my affection for the road, for the smell of jet fuel, for being surrounded by non-English-speaking people. Together, we have explored faraway mountains, cities, islands, seas, and waterways, and regularly alight on Ambridge and Pittsburgh, drawn by family and skin-tight friends.

After long and mostly happy lives, Milt and Betty passed away. I still feel their final kisses on my lips. Betty was buried on a Friday, and the hearse turning into the church parking lot followed a sign that said "Pierogis." In the basement were the women and men with whom she sat shoulder-to-shoulder for years revealing their most private stories while pinching dough. Throughout her life, she gave storytellers her full attention. Their secrets teased her curiosity, which Einstein says has its own reason for existing. Just before her funeral Mass, the pierogi ladies laid down their dough, and, still wearing their floury aprons, filed into the back pews to bid her farewell. The entire sanctuary smelled like butter and onions.

Shortly before he died, Milt marveled at the new grocery store in Ambridge, built on the spot where his father had lost a few fingers. The store rose as a result of Robert Moltoni's company demolishing two hundred acres of decaying mills, attracting light industry and the county's emergency call center.

I am grateful for the promise flickering over my hometown. After meeting Moltoni, my reacquaintance with the place revealed stories I had never heard or had been too self-absorbed to appreciate. Now, when I see industrial rust and ruins like the hollow American Bridge office where my father had bent over a drawing table for thirty years, its present condition seems only temporary. As English writer Christopher Woodward puts it, "[A] ruin is a dialogue between an incomplete reality and the imagination of the spectator." Walking among the eyesores today, I hear echoes of the past and lively conversations about the future.

My family keeps me tied to the tenuous yet enduring belief

that has graced Ambridge from its beginnings. That particular plateau has given birth to grand schemes and redemptive dreams, to fortunes and philosophies, to treachery and charity. Its resources and situation made it fertile ground for growth—economic, industrial, social, spiritual, and personal. Exploitation and greed challenged its survival, but certain resources persisted: The river flows cleaner; the sun still bathes its hills from early morning until dusk, and new arrivals push seeds of their own dreams into its soil.

For three hundred years, western Pennsylvania, like the entire industrial heartland, was shaped by newcomers. To some extent, that's still true. But like never before, its vitality comes from those who have stayed. My friends and family are among them—a compassionate union leader, a prominent journalist, teachers, counselors, investors, restaurateurs, crime fighters, cooks, artists, poets, and a small army that still comes home filthy at the end of a shift. Rescuing the Rust Belt, they are my heroes.

~

Acknowledgments

Special thanks to Eugenia Kim for contributions too broad, deep, and numerous to list, enriching every page of this book.

With gratitude for my teachers and family, especially Maria Vanyo, for reading earliest drafts, for Debra Papadinoff, Page Palmer, Steve Butkus, Pamela Erdmann, Sy Montgomery, Howard Mansfield, Mary Bianchi, MC Sacco, Baxter Harris, Amy Markus, Denise Thomas, Debbie Danielpour, Gail Harrington, Shilo Porter, Greg Connelly, and the provocative David Macy and Ian Meiklejohn. Your kindness and interest have made all the difference to me. And Spooner, thanks for sitting on my feet and leading the way.

With Gratitude

To Edward Flynn and all those named and otherwise portrayed here, whose stories and character have become part of my own story.

To Jane Eklund and the team at Bauhan Publishing.